C for Chemicals

Michael Birkin studied chemistry until the age of 22, when he abandoned the academic world in favour of activism and founded one of the first local Friends of the Earth groups. He has worked as a forester, paper recycler, field survey worker, and environmental campaigner: he is now an environmental consultant, and lives in Bristol. Practising what he preaches, he tends an organic vegetable patch and does not run a car.

Brian Price is a freelance pollution consultant. He wrote *The Friends of the Earth Guide to Pollution* (Maurice Temple Smith, 1983); other work includes studies on lead in playground dust and paint, incineration of hazardous wastes, and pollution in the Severn Estuary, and he is a contributor to *New Scientist* and other journals. He tutors the Open University's Technology Foundation and Environmental Control and Public Health courses. Brian lives in Weston-super-Mare with his wife and two children.

C for Chemicals

Chemical Hazards and How to Avoid Them

Michael Birkin and **Brian Price**

GREEN
PRINT

First published in 1989 by
Green Print
an imprint of The Merlin Press Ltd
10 Malden Road, London NW5 3HR
© Michael Birkin and Brian Price 1989
ISBN 1 85425 027 2
Phototypeset by Input Typesetting Ltd, London
Printed in Great Britain by Biddles, Guildford

CONTENTS

NOTE

The information given in this book is as accurate as we can make it at the time of going to press (February 1989). The contents of specific products and brands may change, and readers should verify this where possible from the labels.

Products and substances are printed in bold in the text when more information may be found in the relevant A–Z listing.

PREFACE

Humanity is currently exposed to a wider range of hazardous chemicals than ever before. Much of this exposure is a result of environmental pollution such as the careless discharge of wastes and the misuse of agricultural chemicals. But some of the problem lies closer to home, as the number of chemicals available to the householder for cleaning, gardening, motoring and do-it-yourself increases by leaps and bounds.

This book is designed to help you sort out which of these chemicals are best avoided in order to protect yourself, your family and the environment. It is not a fanatical 'anti-chemicals' book: nor is it a complacent justification of everything the chemical industry tries to sell us. We acknowledge that chemicals of many kinds, both natural and synthetic, have a major role in modern society, but we do not believe that all the products available are either necessary or safe.

Such is the variety of chemical products in everyday use that we cannot hope to cover every single one in a book of this size. Nor can we read every single paper describing the toxic effects of chemicals that you might encounter. Nevertheless we have tried to cover the major products and have reported on their effects using authoritative sources. We would be very pleased to hear from readers about other products, which could then be included in the next edition. We would also like to hear from people who have additional information on the hazards of relevant materials, whether or not they are discussed here.

We would like to thank Dr Richard Lawson and Jen Morgan (Brian Price's wife) for their invaluable assistance in checking the manuscript for accuracy and sense. Thanks are also due to the staff and volunteers of Avon Friends of the Earth for their support; and to Mary Blake of Friends of the Earth's London Unit, Paul Horsman of the Marine Conservation Society and Vic Simpson, for information supplied. Any errors which remain are, of course, our own.

Mike Birkin
Brian Price
December 1988

1.

INTRODUCTION

It is impossible to avoid chemicals in everyday life. Indeed we ourselves are made up of thousands of complex chemicals, which interact in subtle ways to keep our bodies working. When we use the term 'chemicals', however, we often mean artificial substances used in industry and the home to maintain the standard of living and lifestyle of the (usually) developed world. The term often has a derogatory tone to it, despite the fact that the majority of known substances have minimal or zero adverse effects on health and the environment.

A substance can be viewed in different lights according to its origin — synthetic vanillin is regarded by some people as being inferior to the same material extracted from a vanilla pod despite the fact that there is no difference in chemical terms between them. Someone who swallows three grams of vitamin C (E 300) a day in the hope of warding off colds and cancer may reject the use of ascorbic acid as an antioxidant in food, but the two substances are identical (and both probably came from a factory). The fact that a substance is natural does not guarantee its safety — human ingenuity has not yet managed to create anything as poisonous as some natural chemicals such as ricin and various bacterial toxins.

In this book we concern ourselves with chemicals that, in the main, present hazards to health and environment either when used normally or when misused. As we will see, hundreds of different substances fall into this group and a picture of inadequate regulation, poor safety advice and, in some cases, downright irresponsible marketing will emerge. Some 68,000 chemicals are in use industrially and domestically and two are added to this total nearly every day. A proportion of these are harmless, some are moderately hazardous, a number of them are frankly dangerous and a few are so potentially harmful that only the most skilled handling can prevent a disaster. The consumer is unlikely to encounter this last group, but in the first three categories a number of products are on the market for use in the home. It is these products that form the subject matter of this book.

The main areas covered are household products (cleaners, cosmetics, appliances, furnishings, water, packaging, and toys form the mainstay of this section); garden and greenhouse pesticides and fertilisers; and do-it-yourself products and car accessories, another source of potentially lethal materials. We do not discuss medicines, except in a few instances such as shampoo for killing headlice and some pet products. Nor do we cover the deliberate use of food additives, as this is dealt with comprehensively elsewhere. We exclude radiation hazards, since these are the result of physics rather than chemistry. Nor do we specify those products which have not been tested on animals, although our inclusion of toxicity data based on animal experiments does not mean that we condone all the tests concerned.

In the areas defined above we examine the major types of products available together with some minor but particularly nasty items. We discuss their toxicity (to humans, pets and other animals), any corrosive, irritant or inflammable properties that they may have, and their effects on the environment. Special risks, such as explosions, dangerous combinations with other substances and the potential for allergy induction, are also mentioned. We advise you on how to protect yourself and reduce the risks to the environment, and provide sources of further information.

The book is not a complete course in chemistry or toxicology — it is designed for the average householder, who may have no scientific background at all. In some cases we have had to simplify the science a little to save space and avoid confusion, but we hope that professional scientists will bear with us in this respect in the interests of clarity.

HOW TO USE THE BOOK

The next chapter describes, in general terms, the properties of hazardous chemicals and provides advice on protection, for humans and the environment, against the hazardous effects of chemicals in general. It also demonstrates the shortcomings in the labelling and regulation of household chemicals and highlights the lack of available information concerning some materials.

This is followed by three chapters on the individual groups of products. After a short introductory section the products are listed alphabetically, so you can look up washing powders, slug killers or paint strippers before you buy them. We discuss the general hazards of these products and offer advice on safety precautions, highlighting those materials which, we feel, should not be used.

The individual chemical substances contained in the listed products appear in the A to Z section that forms Chapter 6. Here we give information on the toxicity and other harmful properties, as far as they are known, of all the chemicals mentioned, as well as a few others that you might come across. Special precautions to be observed when handling them are included.

Chapter 7 lists sources of further information such as consultants and official bodies. A bibliography and list of references completes the book.

If you want to find out about the hazards of a product, look it up in the relevant product chapter to find out its likely ingredients and general information about its properties. Then, use the A to Z to find out more about the properties of the ingredients and any special precautions that you should take when using the product. If the names of the ingredients appear on the label you can go straight to the A to Z section, but it is worth reading the product entry as well. Of course, we hope that you will use the book before buying a potentially harmful product and that it will help you in choosing the safest possible option for dealing with a problem.

GLOSSARY OF TERMS

In this section we list a number of abbreviations and technical terms that appear in the book or elsewhere, together with simple explanations of their meanings.

absorption: the soaking up of a liquid or gas into a solution or pores in a solid. Biologically, the taking of something into the body.

acaricide: substance used to kill mites, e.g. the red spider mite.

ACP: Advisory Committee on Pesticides, a government body that advises on pesticide control.

acute toxicity: having toxic effects that appear within a short time of the substance being absorbed.

adsorption: process by which a gas or liquid is held onto the surface of a solid.

allergen: substance capable of causing allergy in certain individuals.

allergy: condition where the body 'switches on' a defensive reaction against a specific substance, often at very low levels of exposure.

anticholinesterase compound: substance that blocks the transmission of nerve messages by affecting a particular enzyme — organophosphorus insecticides fall into this group.

anticoagulant: substance that prevents the blood from clotting.

biocide: substance that kills one or more type of living thing.

biodegradable: substance that can be broken down in the environment by natural (strictly speaking, biological) processes.

broad spectrum: pesticide that kills a wide range of pests.

carcinogen: substance causing cancer.

chronic toxicity: toxic effects that appear over a long period.

corrosive: capable of causing skin burns or damage to metals and other materials.

DOE: Department of the Environment.

embryotoxic: capable of harming an unborn baby in the early stages of development.

enzyme: substance controlling many biochemical processes, e.g. digestion, nerve transmission, manufacture of tissues, in living organisms. Some bacterial enzymes are used in biological detergents.

EPA: Environmental Protection Agency (of the USA).

FAO: Food and Agriculture Organisation.

fetotoxic: harmful to the unborn baby.

formulation: the total mixture in which a pesticide appears, including solvents and materials to make it stick to plants, penetrate tissues, mix with water if necessary etc.

haemoglobin: the red component of blood, which carries oxygen from the lungs to all parts of the body.

HSE: Health and Safety Executive.

IARC: International Agency for Research on Cancer.

ingestion: taking something into the body by mouth.

inorganic: substances not based on carbon, although carbonates and a few gases are also inorganic. In an agricultural context, fertilisers made artificially are inorganic, whatever their composition.

irritant: substance that has painful effects on contact with the skin, ranging from a mild stinging to severe blisters. Some irritants may be corrosive in a concentrated form.

MAFF: Ministry of Agriculture, Fisheries and Foods.

mucous membranes: the delicate moist tissues that line the mouth, nose, throat and breathing passages.

mutagen: substance capable of causing mutations in cells.

narcotic: capable of causing sleepiness.

nematicide: substance used to kill eelworms in the soil.

organic: substances based on carbon, apart from a few inorganic gases and carbonates. Organic farming means farming without artificial fertilisers or pesticides.

persistent: substances that remain in the environment for long periods, e.g. heavy metals and PCBs.

propellant: the compressed gas that drives the product out of an aerosol can when the button is pressed.

residual herbicide: herbicide that leaves active residues in the soil for some time.

secondary poisoning: poisoning of an animal through eating another animal containing toxic material, e.g. pesticides.

selective: pesticide that kills one type of animal or plant but not other, more desirable, types.

sensitiser: substance that initiates an allergy in a person exposed to it.

synergism: process by which the combined effects of two or more substances are greater than the sum of their individual effects.

systemic: (a) affecting the whole body rather than just part of it (for example cyanide is a systemic poison, whereas asbestos normally only affects the lungs).
 (b) an insecticide or fungicide taken into the tissues of a plant and distributed through it so that pests attempting to feed on the plant are poisoned.

teratogen: substance that causes birth defects when absorbed in pregnancy.

translocated: absorbed by one part of a plant and then carried within it to other parts which it affects, leading to the death of the plant.

WHO: World Health Organisation.

2.

PROPERTIES OF CHEMICALS

Exposure to chemicals in daily life is inevitable. Obviously, we can do little to avoid general atmospheric pollutants such as smoke and sulphur dioxide, although we have a responsibility to try to reduce our own contributions to these problems. For example, any form of energy conservation reduces pollution, and by using electricity carefully we save fuel at power stations thereby reducing the amount of acid rain gases or radioactive wastes produced. Ensuring that our motor vehicles run efficiently reduces pollution by exhaust fumes as well as saving energy — and using a bicycle for short journeys is even more effective.

We can, however, have more influence over the nature and quantities of chemicals to which we are exposed in our own homes. We can select the chemical products that pose the least hazard to ourselves and the environment, providing that we know what they contain and what effects the ingredients have. This book can help you to identify the ingredients as well as their potential for harm, but it cannot be completely comprehensive for several reasons.

In the first place, the components of any given type of product may vary, as different manufacturers use various combinations of chemicals for particular purposes. We can tell you what most manufacturers use in, say, deodorants or varnishes, but there may be variations involving more or less hazardous ingredients.

Second, the ingredients may not always be listed on the product's label, although some of the most dangerous products have to be labelled by law (see p. 18). In many cases, where there is no legal requirement to do so, the manufacturers may not be prepared to divulge this information to the consumer or to anyone else. This may be for commercial reasons — they may not wish competitors to learn formulae which could have taken years and a considerable financial investment to develop. This is understandable, but in these days of sophisticated chemical analysis this argument seems rather weak. Manufacturers may also prefer 'not to alarm people' — if a product was found to contain a material that has been the subject of controversy, e.g. a solvent recently accused of being carcinogenic, they would obviously lose sales. One popular argument for maintaining secrecy over the ingredients of a product is that the public would not understand the scientific background to the safety arguments and would act 'irrationally'. Providing the consumer follows the instructions on the label, the argument goes, there should be no problem even if there is a harmful ingredient present. Apart from the fact that people do not always follow the instructions — or may be unable to read the small print — the attitude that scientific uncertainties about safety should be kept from the public is patronising and dangerous.

If you use a product that is potentially harmful, you have a right to know what is in it. If you are allergic to a particular substance you may accidentally expose yourself to a harmful dose of it in a badly labelled product and suffer very unpleasant symptoms as a result. You may also expose other people to the product and cause harm to them inadvertently, especially if they are pregnant or infirm. If there is doubt among experts about the safety of a chemical you should be able to seek independent advice and have a right to choose not to use a product about which you are uncertain. You cannot exercise this right if you do not know what is in the product in the first place and you do not need to be a scientist to decide to 'play safe'.

Of course, you can only choose to avoid a particular ingredient if you can buy a comparable product, or do the job in a different way, without the ingredient in question. This is not always possible. If, in 1980, you wanted to buy a gloss paint that did not contain a lead drier, you would have found it virtually impossible. Until recently, you could not buy a fabric conditioner free from materials likely to cause sensitisation and allergy (see p. 25). Buying a phosphate-free washing powder in the average supermarket is still usually impossible, although some brands are now available through health food shops and similar establishments. In cases like these you are virtually forced to use products that contain potentially harmful materials, since all manufacturers use them.

In seeking to avoid one hazardous material it is important not to create a different hazard with the alternative. Replacing the herbicide 2,4,5-T with ioxynil, for instance, simply exchanges one hazardous chemical for another. Using butane as an aerosol propellant instead of CFCs reduces the risk to the ozone layer but creates a fire hazard in the home. (The answer here, of course, is not to use an aerosol at all). We hope that this book will enable you to weigh up the risks of a product and its alternatives before deciding which to purchase. The ways in which chemicals can be hazardous, to people and to the environment, are the subject of the next section.

WHY CHEMICALS MAY BE HAZARDOUS

A chemical may be hazardous for several different reasons. It may be inflammable, a fire promoter, corrosive and/or poisonous. In addition it may harm the environment, from the ozone layer high above us to marine organisms deep underwater. The hazards of using chemicals can, in many cases, be minimised and problems avoided, but in other cases — e.g. the CFCs currently damaging the ozone layer — the only sensible course of action is to stop using them entirely.

Flammable materials (the word inflammable means the same thing) are simply those that burn easily. Their potential for hazard depends on two factors — how easily they catch fire and what they do when they burn. Many solvents and liquefied gases are highly volatile, which means that they give off large amounts of vapour at low temperatures. If the vapour burns then they present a serious fire risk since a flame, electric spark or glowing cigarette end a long way from the source of the vapour can start a fire.

When gases and some solvents burn they may do so quickly enough to cause an explosion — every year there are several major gas explosions in Britain in which extensive damage to property and, sometimes, loss of life occur. Gases normally burn 'cleanly' in such circumstances and the materials formed as they burn do not contribute greatly to the hazard. The same cannot be said of many plastics and foams in, for instance, furnishings.

Polyurethane foam, used in many items of furniture, emits massive quantities of dense black smoke as well as large amounts of heat when it burns. The smoke contains poisonous gases such as hydrogen cyanide and is the main cause of death in house fires involving such furniture. Very recent foams contain fire retardants, but will still burn given a strong enough source of ignition. Other types of plastic give off different fumes when burning. PVC, for instance, emits the corrosive and poisonous gas hydrogen chloride, as well as small amounts of the highly toxic compounds known as dioxins.

A chemical does not have to burn itself to cause a fire hazard. Some substances, called **oxidising agents**, release oxygen in chemical reactions and make it easier for flammable materials to burn. Examples include the herbicide sodium chlorate and the fertiliser ammonium nitrate. These materials should not be mixed with other substances as they can catch fire with very little provocation — even something as innocuous as sugar can form a potentially explosive mixture with an oxidising agent.

Sometimes a fire can start without any obvious cause; this is known as **spontaneous combustion**. Teak oil and linseed oil thinly spread on rags may heat up and smoulder, eventually bursting into flame, as they react with oxygen in the air. Rags used with oils of this type should be soaked in water before disposal.

There are types of burns other than those caused by heat. Corrosive chemicals can burn the skin and any other tissues with which they come into contact. Hydrochloric and sulphuric acids, and alkalis such as sodium hydroxide, are well known for causing burns, but phenols, hydrogen peroxide and some solvents can, in concentrated form, cause similar harm to tissues. Corrosive chemicals will often damage other materials as well — acids will attack many metals, while some fabrics may be eaten away by acids, alkalis, hydrogen peroxide and bleach.

More dilute solutions of these chemicals, and many other substances, may simply irritate the skin rather than cause serious burns. If someone is allergic to a particular substance the skin may become seriously inflamed after even a small exposure; the condition is known as **dermatitis** or **eczema**. Solvents, alkalis, and detergents that remove the skin's natural oils often cause skin irritation and/or dermatitis, but physical irritation (e.g. by glass fibre particles) can produce the same effect. The degree of skin irritation varies from person to person — some people can develop tolerance to these materials. Those who are allergic to chemicals of this nature should avoid contact with them completely, since any exposure can result in symptoms.

Many chemicals are, of course, poisonous if swallowed, either because of their corrosive effect on the throat and stomach or because they interfere with the thousands of biochemical processes that keep our bodies working properly. If a substance has a rapid effect when swallowed (or absorbed by any other route) it is said to be **acutely toxic**. If its effects are felt over a long period of time it is said to be **chronically toxic**. Cyanides, for instance, are acutely toxic, while repeated exposure to the solvent benzene can cause chronic poisoning. Many poisons can act both acutely or chronically depending on the dose — a large dose of mercury compound will kill you quickly, whereas a series of smaller doses or continuous low-level exposure can lead to chronic mercury poisoning.

Household chemicals are rarely swallowed deliberately except by children who taste carelessly stored cleaning products etc. But we can swallow chemicals by accident either through carelessness or as a consequence of their normal use. Many people have died as a result of accidentally drinking pesticides stored in soft drink containers — a dangerous and illegal practice. People eating, drinking or smoking while using toxic substances run the risk of transferring material from their fingers to their mouths. Dust — for instance from lead paint removal — can contaminate food and the surfaces upon which it is prepared and eaten.

Chemicals can get into our bodies in ways other than by swallowing. Our lungs are very efficient at extracting materials from the air, including toxic vapours, gases and dusts. These are readily absorbed into the bloodstream and carried to parts of the body where they can do harm, e.g. the brain, heart and liver. Some dusts, such as asbestos and silica, may remain in the lungs and cause trouble there, e.g. by causing asbestosis or lung cancer. Others may be carried out of the lungs by the action of the tiny hairs that line the breathing passages. They are then swallowed, possibly to be absorbed in the digestive system.

The third way in which chemicals can enter the body is through the skin. Many organic compounds, especially those which dissolve in oils, can penetrate the skin and enter the bloodstream. Lead from dust has been found to pass through intact skin and the highly toxic lead compound used in leaded petrol (tetraethyl lead) goes through skin very easily.

Once in the bloodstream, whether it enters via the lungs, skin or gut, a toxic chemical is in a position to do harm. In some cases the blood itself is the target — carbon monoxide and nitrites, for instance, bind to the haemoglobin in the red blood cells and prevent it from carrying vital oxygen to the tissues. The nervous system, especially the brain, is sensitive to attack by many substances. Lead and mercury can cause brain damage, some solvents can cause narcosis (sleepiness) when they reach the brain, and many insecticides can disrupt the process by which nerves carry messages to and from the brain, thereby disrupting many vital systems. The heart is affected, directly or indirectly, by solvents, pesticides and many plant products (e.g. nicotine), while the liver and kidneys can be damaged by cadmium, some solvents and a variety of pesticides.

One effect that many chemicals can have is the production of cancer, a process called **carcinogenesis**. A cancer is a group of cells that grows out of control and invades the tissues, eventually causing death. Exactly how a cancer starts is not understood, but it is thought to involve a complex pattern of heredity, lifestyle, environmental factors and pure chance. Many chemicals are known carcinogens — arsenic, asbestos and benzene to name but three — and many more are suspected of causing cancer. In most cases direct evidence of cancer caused by chemicals in humans is difficult to come by. All we can do is compare groups of people exposed to a substance with similar people not exposed to it in order to see whether there is a difference in cancer rates that can be attributed to the chemical. This is very difficult to do, as people are often exposed to many possible carcinogens at the same time and have varying lifestyles. Toxicity assessments normally rely on experiments on animals — usually rats, mice and rabbits — and it is assumed that something that does not cause cancer in these species is unlikely to be carcinogenic in humans. Sometimes this parallel breaks down and there is disagreement among scientists about cancer risks — in the USA if a material causes cancer in mice it is regarded as likely to do so in humans. British authorities do not always accept this, which is why the insecticide dieldrin was allowed to be used in Britain long after it was banned as a carcinogen in the United States.

A more subtle and equally devastating way in which chemicals can interfere with life processes is by causing mutations and birth defects. Human development in the uterus is controlled by genetic 'instructions' in our cells. These instructions can be disrupted if a pregnant woman is exposed to certain substances or to radiation. Chemicals capable of having this effect are known as **teratogens** — the most infamous reported teratogen is the drug thalidomide. Other substances, including some heavy metals, pesticides and alcohol, are now suspected teratogens. Some birth defects may result from the father's exposure to chemicals — men exposed to large quantities of hydrocarbons in their work seem to father more children with a rare genetic defect (Prader–Willi syndrome), although at this stage in research the evidence is not conclusive. Scientific debate is still raging over whether the use of herbicides to destroy crops and jungle by US and Australian servicemen in Vietnam led to their fathering deformed children as a result. Some chemicals are known to reduce male fertility.

The developing foetus — and the sperm and egg cells that fuse to begin the formation of the embryo — are particularly vulnerable to the effects of harmful chemicals. But they are not the only stages of the human lifecycle where special care is needed. Babies and young children are also special risk groups, especially as far as inhaled chemicals are concerned. Because babies' lungs are immature, and they breathe more air in relation to their body weight than do older people, they can be harmed by levels of air pollution that their parents would hardly notice.

Young babies are also more susceptible to ingested (swallowed) poisons — nitrate is particularly dangerous during the first six months of life since it is easily converted into nitrite by the immature digestive system. Also, nitrite combines more readily with the young infant's blood than it does with that of an older child. The result is a type of internal suffocation called methaemoglobinaemia or 'blue baby syndrome'.

Elderly people, especially those with lung or heart problems, should take special care to avoid breathing toxic chemicals. Anything that irritates the lungs is also likely to put an increased strain on the heart, and such strain is best avoided in later life. People suffering from asthma, bronchitis or other respiratory illnesses should also be careful — isocyanates and many dusty materials can aggravate their condition, sometimes very seriously.

Some individuals have particularly strong reactions to small amounts of a substance. This is called **allergy** — the body's defence mechanisms over-react, producing a wide range of symptoms from skin itching to severe breathing problems, depending on how the chemical is absorbed. Isocyanates have this effect on some people, and initial exposure to a chemical of this type may cause sensitisation. A person who is sensitised to a chemical suffers ill effects from an initial, moderately large exposure, but if they then encounter even small doses of the chemical again they suffer symptoms out of all proportion to the exposure — in other words, they become allergic to it.

Other individuals react very strongly to a group of chemicals known as **anticholinesterase agents**. This group includes insecticides of the organophosphorus and carbamate type, as well as some medicinal products. The chemicals interfere with the transmission of messages by the nerves and those affected suffer from trembling, headaches and weakness, and sometimes collapse after even quite small exposures. Susceptibility to anticholinesterase agents is a well-known phenomenon and some products carry warnings to the effect that sensitive individuals should avoid using the products. Less well documented is the possibility that repeated exposure to small doses of these materials, particularly insecticides used in agriculture, may cause low-level and vague nervous symptoms in otherwise healthy people.

When safety limits for chemicals are set they are usually based on the industrial situation. It is assumed that the people using them will be male, aged 18–60, reasonably healthy and exposed for only eight hours per day. Industrial limits do not normally cater for the protection of pregnant women, small children, the elderly or the infirm. The safety warnings on the product labels usually reflect this. Neither is exposure for longer than eight hours per day taken into account, yet a house that is being painted by enthusiastic do-it-yourselfers may contain high levels of solvents in the atmosphere twenty-four hours per day for several weeks.

Of course, humans are not the only species at risk from household chemicals. Pets can be harmed by the careless use of these materials and cats are particularly at risk from organochlorine compounds. Cats cannot break down this type of chemical in their livers — unlike many other species — hence continuous exposure to small quantities can cause a build-up of poison to lethal levels. Cats can die through being put in a room in which the floor has been treated with an organochlorine insecticide for woodworm but has not been covered afterwards. They pick up small amounts of insecticide from the floor and are poisoned by it. Dogs put in the same room would probably not be harmed. Such insecticides pose a long-term hazard to cats and also to bats (if used in lofts). Cats also tend to eat slug pellets in the garden unless the pellets are treated with a cat repellant.

Fish are very susceptible to poisoning, especially by pesticides. Their gills can extract toxic chemicals from the water very efficiently, and cause the chemicals to build up in their tissues to dangerous levels. Fish tanks and fish ponds should always be covered if chemicals are used in their vicinity — portable tanks and bowls should be removed from the room if possible. Pesticides are also very dangerous to bees, which can carry a lethal dose of insecticide back to the hive in collected pollen.

Almost everything we do has an impact on the wider environment. When we buy an item it has already had an effect, since its manufacture and transport has involved the use of resources, energy and — usually — the creation of pollution. When we use the product we may also cause pollution and perhaps use energy; the conversion of energy nearly always creates pollution. Finally, when we dispose of something that, too, can pollute the environment. This pollution may be immediate and obvious — discarding a pesticide container or used motor oil into a stream will produce a damaging effect almost at once. Other instances are more subtle and insidious, like the damage caused to the protective ozone layer high above us by the use of CFCs in foams and aerosols.

Some pollutants — e.g. sewage — are largely biodegradable and break down in the environment. This does not mean that they are not harmful, merely that their potential for harm does not remain indefinitely. Many of the worst pollution problems are caused by persistent materials such as organochlorine compounds and heavy metals. These do not break down in the environment and may accumulate in the tissues of plants and animals. As one animal eats another the residues are passed on to the next in line and the species at the top of this 'food chain' may be affected fatally. This happened with the chemicals aldrin and dieldrin, which affected birds of prey in Britain in the 1950s and it is still believed to be happening with PCBs and seals in parts of the North Sea today — despite the fact that the dangers from PCBs were first discovered in the late 1960s.

Some of the worst persistent pollutants are no longer used on a wide scale in Britain, but the illicit use of some, such as DDT, probably still goes on. Heavy metals are still used widely, however, and at the time of writing the vast majority of petrol sold in Britain is leaded. Residues of past persistent pollutant use remain and will continue to do so for many years.

Many non-persistent pollutants cause serious damage as well. Phosphates from detergents in sewage entering vulnerable waterways are rapidly absorbed and changed by tiny plants, causing a massive overgrowth and the loss of all the dissolved oxygen in the water — a process called **eutrophication**. The same phenomenon can happen with nitrates from fertiliser use. The fumes emitted from car exhausts are rapidly changed into other substances, but these can then be harmful, causing air pollution and acid deposition. For instance, hydrocarbons and nitrogen oxides react with sunlight and oxygen to produce the powerful irritant ozone, a component of the notorious Los Angeles smogs. Modern non-persistent insecticides may leave no residues, but they can have a devastating effect on non-target species, even when used properly.

Chemical safety problems are often complicated by the fact that we may be dealing with a mixture of chemicals rather than a pure substance. Chemicals may react together in the environment to produce other, possibly more harmful, substances. This happens with car exhaust fumes as mentioned above, but can also occur with household chemicals. Acids added to bleach will release highly toxic chlorine gas, while acids mixed with sodium chlorate weedkiller can cause a fire, if not an explosion. If bleach is spilt near to where wood fillers containing styrene are in use, vapours of chlorostyrene may be formed and these are powerfully irritating to the eyes.

The combined effects of two or more substances on the body may be greater than the sum of their individual effects, a process called **synergism**. This phenomenon is exploited in some insecticides — pyrethrin is a moderately effective fly-killer and piperonyl butoxide has little effect on insects. If the two are mixed the resulting combination is powerfully insecticidal. The fungicide thiram is moderately toxic to humans but a small dose will produce no noticeable effects. If someone who has absorbed a small dose then drinks a little alcohol they will feel extremely sick — an interaction used in the treatment of alcoholism with a drug very similar to thiram. The combined effects of mixtures of chemicals are very difficult to predict, especially when many chemicals are involved and symptoms are likely to be vague. We just do not know whether or not people are suffering minor but prolonged health problems from the combined effects of chemicals inside and outside the home, although there is a growing body of medical and quasi-medical opinion that suggests this may be the case.

A major problem in this area is that we do not have enough information about the individual chemicals. This ignorance may take two forms. In many cases no-one really knows what the hazards are, and chemicals have been used on a widespread basis before the risks became apparent. Asbestos, for example, was used for centuries before its dangers were appreciated and we are still learning about it.

The other information gap results from some people being aware of the dangers but not revealing their knowledge. Asbestos, again, is a good example, since some of the companies handling it suppressed important evidence about its lethal properties for decades.

Currently, any new chemical coming onto the market in quantities of one tonne or more per year must be tested. The results of these tests, on its physical, chemical and toxicological properties, must be sent to the Health and Safety Executive. The producer does not have to divulge this information to anyone else and will rarely do so. In the case of new pesticides, data are available for inspection by the public, but copies are not supplied and you cannot take notes. Manufacturers of products used industrially are obliged to provide data sheets to workers on the hazards of the materials concerned, but these are often inadequate. They are not required to supply this information to the householder or do-it-yourself enthusiast.

Container labels should be a reliable source of information, but this is not always the case. By law, larger packs of many substances should carry details of the contents and appropriate safety warnings. This rule does not apply to small containers or complex mixtures — hence many DIY and household products have only vague or non-existent descriptions of their contents on the label. All pesticides have to be properly labelled, however. A responsible manufacturer will put comprehensive guidance and safety warnings on the container, but the quality of this advice is variable. Different brands of essentially the same type of product may carry very different advice.

PROTECTING YOURSELF AND THE ENVIRONMENT

The first rule for protecting yourself and the environment against the effects of chemicals in the home is to ask yourself 'Is the product necessary?' In many instances a particular product may not be essential and an alternative means of tackling a problem can be found — it is safer and more effective to mend a leaky drainpipe, for instance, than to coat the inside of a wall with an isocyanate-containing damp sealant. The occasional fly can be swatted or caught on sticky flypaper rather than sprayed, thereby avoiding the release of an insecticide into the whole room and also preventing damage to the ozone layer if the spray contains CFCs.

If there is no alternative to a chemical product the next question is 'Is this the safest and least environmentally damaging product I can use?' When cleaning a dirty oven a cream or paste is safer than a caustic spray. A pyrethrin-based wasp killer is safer than one based on lindane. A hand-sprayed windscreen de-icer based on isopropanol is safer than an aerosol containing methanol — and a fish slice is even safer! In fact, almost anything in an aerosol container can and should be replaced by another product. Aerosols not only damage the ozone layer with their propellants (although this is changing), but also represent a tremendous waste of resources, pose a hazard when discarded and may burst or explode if accidentally heated. In addition, they are less controllable than a paste or a brushed product.

If you have to use a potentially harmful chemical product there are several steps you can take to protect yourself. First, always use the minimum quantity to do the job — overdosing the detergent or wood preserver not only wastes money, it increases any risk. Second, read and follow the instructions and warnings on the label. They may be inaccurate and incomplete but they are a starting point. Third, check in the product guide and the A–Z sections of this book to see if there are additional precautions that you should take.

Never swallow or taste household chemicals. Do not smoke, eat or drink while using hazardous materials. Cigarettes can obviously ignite flammable materials, but they also convert some chlorinated hydrocarbon solvents into the war gas phosgene as the solvent is drawn through the burning tobacco. Pilot lights in gas appliances can ignite inflammable gases and vapours — in one documented instance the solvent vapours from adhesive being used to lay cork tiles caught fire when they drifted onto a boiler pilot light.

Store household chemicals away from food and in the original containers. Re-label them if the original labels become obscured. Ensure that children do not get hold of them — some children are likely to taste anything they come across. A child may like the hiss of an aerosol can, having seen an adult use one or played with 'aerosol string', but if the child grabs a spray oven cleaner the results could be horrific. Buy products in child-safe containers where possible.

Keep chemical products off your skin, especially those listed as irritant, corrosive, harmful or toxic. Woollen gloves are useless, as they will keep out neither liquids nor dusts. The thin plastic gloves used for medical purposes break if used roughly and a leaky glove is worse than useless since material becomes trapped against your skin. Make sure that the gloves you intend to use do not dissolve in the product in question.

When using solvent-based products — or any others that emit harmful vapours — ensure that you work in well-ventilated conditions. If you start to feel drowsy or experience a tightening in the chest or coughing, leave the job and get some fresh air. If you are using large quantities of solvent-based material, especially in a confined space, such as when treating lofts against woodworm, wear a proper industrial breathing mask — the local office of the Health and Safety Executive should be able to advise you of the appropriate type and may know of a local supplier. Simple 'Martindale' type dust masks are widely available from DIY shops and can protect you against dusts such as sawdust and cement — use these for dusty jobs. They will not protect you against vapours, gases, asbestos or very fine dusts.

Eye protection is vital when using corrosive materials, power tools or paints and pesticides in sprays. Brushing liquids at head height, on ceilings etc. can easily lead to droplets getting into your eyes especially if the surface is rough. If you wear glasses you will obviously get some protection, but splashes and spray mist can get around the sides. Proper eye protection is shaped to fit closely to the contours of your face all the way round, and is made of tough plastic rather than glass.

When handling pesticides, wood treatments, doing dusty jobs and otherwise exposing yourself to substantial contamination you should wear rough clothes which cover you virtually completely — do not wear shorts and a T-shirt when splashing wood preserver around, for instance. Clothing should be easy to remove if it becomes contaminated — pulling a tight jumper soaked in bitumen over your head could wipe the material over your face and into your eyes. Acids and strong alkalis can eat their way through clothing, and some synthetic materials will dissolve in certain organic solvents, so be alert to the effects of splashes. Remove dusty or splashed clothing before re-entering the living area of the house in order to prevent contamination of food, furnishings and other people.

If you feel unwell after using a chemical product, try to avoid any further exposure to it, e.g. do not sleep in a recently painted bedroom if you think that painting it has made you ill. Seek medical advice and be prepared to tell your doctor exactly what you used, when you used it and when the symptoms began to appear. Some doctors may be dismissive or unhelpful but if you feel you have a long-term problem you can ask to be referred to a specialist, and you have the right to a second opinion.

One final point: if you are trying to conceive, are pregnant, or think you may be, take especial care to avoid exposure to chemicals, particularly during the first three months. Some substances — e.g. certain pesticides — are known to harm the developing foetus in animals. We simply do not know if these — or many other chemicals in common use — can also produce birth defects in humans.

3.

HOUSEHOLD PRODUCTS

APPLIANCES

Batteries

How would you behave if appliances such as cameras, calculators and toys were powered by tiny nuclear reactors? When they were spent, would you throw your little packets of personal nuclear waste in the dustbin without a second thought? Most people probably wouldn't, but in fact of all the materials which the human race adds to the environment every year, the combined toxicity of metals considerably exceeds that from radioactive waste. Here we do indeed add our personal contributions to this toxic burden, in the form of batteries that may contain several different metals, including such highly toxic ones as **mercury** and **cadmium**.

Mercury is contained in button cells for applications such as cameras, hearing aids and some toys. Disposal of these is the most significant way in which householders may pollute the environment with this metal. Mercury in household refuse can contribute to air pollution if it ends up in an incinerator or to water pollution if it goes to a landfill site. In the latter case the mercury may be converted in the tip to the very hazardous methyl mercury before oozing out if the tip is not securely sealed.

The commonest form of battery is the zinc–carbon type, which is much less of a pollution problem. The longer-lasting alkaline batteries are rather more hazardous but if they are used correctly fewer should be needed.

Rechargeable batteries are made of nickel and cadmium. Cadmium is extremely toxic, but with careful use far fewer of them should need to be disposed of; they may last several hundred times longer than the zinc–carbon type.

To reduce your household's pollution burden consider first, where safety permits, replacing batteries with a transformer linked into the mains. This is a sound practice anyway, as it not only saves you money but it is saving energy too. The manufacture of batteries consumes far more energy than you ever get out of them. Second, make sure that you use the right kind of battery for the purpose and do not use it wastefully.

The collection of batteries for recycling or disposal in a 'special waste facility' is now an established practice in some continental countries, but it is as yet uncommon here. Health authorities may collect used hearing aid batteries, but camera shops and the like do not. You might write to the manufacturers and ask if they are willing to set up collection schemes. At least one manufacturer says they will take mercury cells back, but this is of limited use while there are no obvious places where you can return the batteries. Until such schemes do exist, the dustbin is the best option. Never throw any kind of used battery on a fire; as well as the risk from toxic vapours they may explode. Take care not to puncture any batteries and so allow their contents to leak out.

Mercury-free cells are apparently available in other countries. It is perhaps also worth pestering the manufacturers to explain why they are not available here.

Cooking utensils
Most lightweight saucepans are made from **aluminium**. Since a high aluminium intake has been linked with Alzheimer's disease and other mental disorders (see the entry in Chapter 6), some people feel that aluminium vessels should be avoided. Aluminium is however not very easy to dissolve, and unless you are cooking highly acidic foods such as rhubarb, tomatoes or chutneys the amount that gets into food from cooking utensils is not likely to be significant.

Red or orange-enamelled utensils may contain **cadmium**. Older cookware may contain more and, if it is chipped or cracked, it may leach out more readily.

Fluorescent lights
Fluorescent light tubes contain small amounts of **mercury** compounds. Take care not to break them when they need replacing; put them in the packaging from the new tube and leave them out intact for collection with the household waste.

The small capacitors that are used as starters may need replacing as well from time to time. These used to be made with **PCBs**, which are highly toxic, so be very careful not to break one. There are no special arrangements in Britain for collection of small amounts of toxic materials such as this, though in other countries reception facilities have been set up.

Gas appliances

There are several hazards associated with the use of gas cookers, room heaters etc., whether they use bottled gas or mains. The most obvious danger is the risk of explosion if any gas should leak. Propane, butane and natural gas can all form explosive mixtures with air. If you detect a gas leak, then you must put out any naked lights and open all windows and doors at once. Do not switch any electrical device on or off, as the spark may be sufficient to set off an explosion.

A more insidious threat, and one that claims hundreds of lives every year, is poisoning by the **carbon monoxide** that forms if the appliance is not burning gas efficiently. It is essential that stoves and heating systems are properly maintained so that they have enough air and the flue gases can escape.

The burning of any fuel produces **nitrogen oxides** in the air, and while these gases will not build up to a level where they are acutely toxic, there may be a long-term risk to health in poorly ventilated rooms. Small kitchens especially are areas where nitrogen oxides may reach high levels, and you should consider fitting an extractor fan. Nitrogen oxides may lower your resistance to infections of the throat and respiratory tract, and there is evidence that they may aggravate your condition if you are asthmatic.

Refrigerators

Nearly all modern refrigerators contain **chlorofluorocarbons** (CFCs) as the working fluid. In normal use this should present no problems, as the heat exchanger is a sealed unit and no fluid should escape. The danger is that CFCs will be released into the atmosphere when the refrigerator needs replacing. At present there are no arrangements for collecting and recycling the CFCs from old domestic refrigerators and it is to be hoped that this will soon change. Until it does the best policy is simply not to buy a new refrigerator unless you really have to. Write to the manufacturers and tell them why not! If you do buy a new refrigerator check the Consumers' Association reports and choose a model that will last. Alternative fluids that have been used include **ammonia**; few refrigerators use this nowadays as CFCs are cheap and efficient by comparison and ammonia is a toxic and irritant gas that would be dangerous if it escaped. In the longer term new CFC products are being developed that do not threaten the ozone layer so much. They are being produced on a pilot scale now and tested for toxicity and it is hoped that these will prove acceptable substitutes.

Thermometers
The older type of clinical thermometer contains **mercury**, which may become a toxic hazard if the thermometer breaks and mercury is allowed to vaporise. If this happens clean up as instructed under the heading 'Mercury' in Chapter 6. When buying a new thermometer you can avoid this risk altogether by choosing one of the digital or strip types, which do not contain mercury.

CLEANING PRODUCTS

Air fresheners
Supermarket shelves are crammed with these products, and 'fresheners' and perfumes are also added to detergents, fabric conditioners, carpet shampoos, soap, hair lacquer, insecticides, deodorants and so on. The odours of a modern home may be totally synthetic, and this is not without its risks. The substances used include various hydrocarbons, such as limonene, and imidazoline. Some just have a pleasant odour, but others work by a blocking effect, reducing your ability to smell what is really in the air. Little is known about the toxicology of these compounds, but some people have an intolerance of hydrocarbons in general. Limonene, which provides the 'lemon' smell in many products, is a possible animal carcinogen. There are other subtle risks in the use of such products in your home. They may mask, or prevent you from smelling, something that you really ought to be able to smell, such as mouldy food, generally 'stale' air or

even a gas leak. These all have risks for your health and you
would be better off knowing about them. The inability to smell
may have emotional side-effects too: one doctor in Avon has
collected details of fifty cases of patients who complained of
feelings of 'muzziness' and 'unreality' that disappeared on ban-
ishing air fresheners from their homes! Alternative methods of
reducing unpleasant odours in your home include plant materials
such as dried lavender and mint leaves. Burning a candle helps
dispel stale cigarette smoke. If you have a separate kitchen waste
bin for compostable materials then put a small amount of dry
peat or granules such as 'perlite' in the bottom of the bin and it
will prevent odours from the liquid that may ooze out of bin
liners. Grow a scented plant. Open the window!

Bleaches and disinfectants

There are two standard types of bleach. There are the 'chlorine'
ones; **sodium hypochlorite** is the familiar liquid bleach, 'bleaching powder' is **calcium hypochlorite**. Although they have a
distinct chlorine smell and can liberate **chlorine** gas if they are
accidentally mixed with acids, the way they kill bacteria is to
produce reactive oxygen in the water. Their chemical action is
thus not that different from the 'oxygen' or 'peroxide' bleaches.
Hydrogen peroxide itself is the strongest of these, strong
enough in fact to bleach wood. More often a chemical such as
sodium percarbonate is used, which generates a certain amount
of peroxide once it is dissolved. These kinds are used in stain
removers and some detergents. The toxicity of bleaches varies —
see the individual entries in Chapter 6 — but all should be
treated with caution. Keep them off your skin and out of your
eyes and do not leave them where a child might experimentally
swallow some. If any bleach product is swallowed then rinse out
the mouth with plenty of water and drink a lot of water or milk.
See a doctor as soon as possible.

The oxygen bleaches are less harsh for use on fabric. If you
need a bleach for an outdoor job such as cleaning algae off a
path, then bleaching powder is a somewhat milder product than
sodium hypochlorite. The manufacturers of bleach encourage
you to pour it down sinks, toilets and drains at frequent intervals.
Unless you have a specific problem there is no point in doing

this; you are merely creating difficulties for the bacteria that break down sewage. If you have a septic tank you should not do it at all.

For disinfectant purposes milder products based on **quaternary ammonium compounds** are available. It is important to remember that the word 'disinfectant' covers a multitude of products ranging from harsh phenolic compounds for pouring down drains to medicinal products which may, when safely diluted, be applied to skin. All disinfectants should however be treated as potentially toxic materials, especially where children are concerned. If treating a cat or any bedding it may use with a disinfectant, remember that chlorinated hydrocarbons are uniquely poisonous to cats and this rules out the use of some products.

De-scalers
These are chemicals for removing the deposits that build up on baths, sinks and toilets or in kettles, especially in hard water areas. Most are based on an acid.

The kettle de-scalers are usually **formic** or **sulphamic acid**. Both are corrosive chemicals, which must be kept off the skin and out of the eyes, and are toxic if swallowed. Formic acid also has a highly irritating vapour. Dilute the chemical for use as recommended and do not peer into kettles to see how well the process is going, as irritant fumes will be given off by the acid as it attacks the scale.

Some de-scalers are advertised as acid-free and biodegradable. As they do not say what they do contain we are unable to comment on these claims.

De-scalers or 'shiners' for sinks and baths include products based on **citric** and **phosphoric acids**. Citric acid is relatively mild but it is a skin irritant and potential allergen; wear gloves when using it and keep it out of your eyes. Phosphoric acid is altogether more dangerous and an accident with this chemical could result in serious skin or eye injury.

Detergents
The usual detergent product, whatever its purpose, contains **phosphates** and surfactants. The surfactants remove grease and

particles of dirt from the object to be cleaned and the phosphates act mainly as water-softeners. Many other ingredients may be added, especially to washing powders.

The use of surfactants resulted in serious environmental problems in the 1960s. Piles of foam, sometimes many feet thick, could be seen at the outlets from sewage works. The detergent industry then reached a voluntary agreement to change the surfactants used to more biodegradable ones. Even so, problems do remain in some areas. The main difficulty now is with phosphates, which are plant nutrients and can stimulate the growth of algae in lakes and rivers, removing oxygen from the waters. Such algal 'blooms' may result in the eventual suffocation of fish. It is estimated that at least 25 per cent of the phosphate added to fresh water in Britain comes from detergents.

Adding phosphate to fresh water, however, will only cause ecological problems in certain circumstances. If the algae are restricted in their growth because the water is muddy and they do not get enough light, or because they are short of some other nutrient such as nitrate, then merely adding more phosphate will make no difference at all. So it seems that in fact relatively few areas of inland Britain — chiefly the Norfolk Broads and Lough Neagh — are at risk from phosphate pollution of the waters.

There may be pressure on Britain to reduce the flow of phosphates into the North Sea, although some feel this is a matter of politics as much as it is of pollution. The input of phosphates from English rivers is very small compared with that from the Continental North Sea states. Overall it seems that the case for phosphate-free detergents is often overstated.

The detergent industry has argued that phosphate-free detergents are simply not as effective. Now that Sainsbury have become the first supermarket chain to stock 'Ecover' phosphate-free washing powder and have announced that it has passed their quality control tests this argument begins to look rather weak.

Other ingredients of detergents that may be cause for concern are enzymes, bleaches, perfumes and optical brighteners. All are largely unnecessary. Enzymes have attracted some adverse publicity because they have caused dermatitis and allergic reactions in sensitive people. Do not use enzyme-containing ('biological') detergents if you have a sensitive skin, and in any case always wear gloves when using them.

The other additives have a generally low degree of biodegradability. The manufacturers of 'Ecover' state that residual traces of optical brightener and perfume may be harmful to fish but we have not been able to check these claims.

All detergents are potential skin irritants; they remove oils from the skin and can cause it to crack or become inflamed. If you are in frequent or prolonged contact with detergent solutions then you should wear gloves. There is a possibility that detergent residues may upset the delicate digestive system of very young children; babies' feeding bottles etc. should be thoroughly rinsed after washing.

Fabric conditioners
See Air fresheners.

Oven cleaners
Most oven cleaners are based on **sodium hydroxide** (caustic soda or sometimes simply 'caustic'), a corrosive and irritant chemical that is highly toxic if swallowed and potentially dangerous to the eyes. Aerosols containing sodium hydroxide are particularly hazardous and we do not feel there is any place for these in the home. Caustic products are really only necessary for heavy deposits of burnt-on spills and their use is best avoided if possible. Try baking soda first: moisten the spill and sprinkle on baking soda, remove with an ordinary pan scrubber, or fine steel wool for tough spots. Check the manufacturer's instructions however, as 'self-cleaning' oven surfaces may be damaged by steel wool. A warm washing soda solution or an ordinary detergent may be used for routine cleaning. If a casserole or the like has spilt inside the oven then sprinkle salt on the spill while it is still warm; it should then be easier to scrub off when cool. Wear rubber gloves for any of these jobs to avoid skin irritation; detergents remove the natural oils and dry out your skin and washing soda can take off the outer layer of skin itself. Take care not to splash washing soda in your eyes.

These precautions of course apply even more strongly in the case of sodium hydroxide. If you do find you need to use a caustic stick or pad then use the lowest concentration you can find. Wipe and then wash it off thoroughly and with as much care as when you put it on. Dispose of the finished pad carefully, wrapping it up in old papers before putting it in the bin. Sodium hydroxide may react strongly with other household cleaners, particularly acids or ammonia solution (with the latter, clouds of toxic **ammonia gas** may be released), so keep other products well away when you are using it.

Some specialist cleaners are marketed for use in microwave ovens. These contain fungicides and bactericides as well as detergents. They were recently tested by the Consumers' Association who found them to be no better than ordinary detergent in warm water. The extra biocidal ingredients should be quite unnecessary if the inside of the microwave is kept routinely clean (you should do this anyway as there is some risk of fire in a dirty microwave oven).

Stain removers

A variety of products is available to tackle stains. Most are based on **solvents**, either singly or in mixtures, although some have a mild bleach such as **sodium percarbonate**. The constituents of stain removers are usually printed on the containers so you can use our A–Z guide to check for the hazards that may be associated with their use. You should avoid breathing solvent vapours when using any of these products and keep them away from your skin and eyes as some may be severe irritants. They may be inflammable too. Overall, **trichloroethane** is probably the least hazardous of the solvents on offer.

You probably only need to use a solvent product to remove greasy stains. Most other stains can be tackled using detergent in warm water or a traditional remedy such as baking soda or salt (but salt should not be used on a carpet). For stains on clothing the simplest remedy is to machine or hand wash. Getting the stained item into cold water as soon as possible increases your chance of success.

Toilet cleaners

Most toilet bowl cleaners are based on an acidic material, usually **sodium hydrogen sulphate**. These are potentially very irritant to the skin, mouth, eyes and mucous membranes. Wear gloves when using them and avoid breathing any dust. Take care to store such products where children cannot reach them. Never mix any two toilet cleaners; if the acidic kind comes into contact with bleach then a violent reaction may ensue and clouds of highly toxic **chlorine** gas will be released. Accidents of this kind are potentially fatal.

Ecover now market a toilet cleaner based on 'natural' **acetic acid**. The toxicity of acetic acid depends on how strong it is and what you do with it; whether or not it is 'natural' is irrelevant! The acidity of this product seems comparatively mild, but the solution may still irritate the skin if spilt. The same precautions apply as with other toilet cleaners.

Toilet freshener blocks for suspending in the bowl or the cistern often contain **paradichlorobenzene**, a chlorinated hydrocarbon that is carcinogenic in animals and has been linked to liver disorders in chronically exposed people. It is a persistent contaminant of water and sewage sludge and its widespread release into the environment should be avoided: do not use these products.

Window cleaners

Some window cleaners contain **white spirit**, which can irritate the skin and is moderately toxic if swallowed or inhaled. Keep these products off your skin and use in well-ventilated conditions. Store where children cannot get at them.

COSMETICS AND TOILETRIES

Deodorants

Many deodorant products are based on **aluminium chlorohydrate**, an irritant chemical. It should not be used if you have a cracked or sensitive skin. The substance is irritating to the eyes and aerosol products therefore present more of a risk: you are hardly likely to get it in your eyes with a roll-on or a stick!

Other deodorants on offer are based on zirconium compounds. In general these seem to be of low toxicity but again they are potentially irritant and should not be used on cracked skin.

Hair care products

A large number of different chemicals are used in hair dyes, many of which are **aromatic compounds**. The list is known to include several allergens and sensitisers and some animal carcinogens as well. As there is no requirement for the manufacturers to state ingredients on sprays and dyes we are unable to advise you on which particular ones to avoid. General precautions include sparing use of such products, not using them if you have cracked or sensitive skin or any broken skin on your scalp, taking great care not to get sprays in your eyes or inhale any of the mist and the use of gloves when massaging products into the scalp. Some of these chemicals may be absorbed through your skin so it is generally unwise to use them in the bath because they will have a lot more skin to get to work on, and at higher temperatures they may pass through the skin more easily.

Perm solutions frequently contain **ammonium thioglycollate**, which is a strong allergen and may cause contact dermatitis. This is one ingredient that is sometimes labelled, as it is particularly important for sensitive people to avoid it.

Some shampoos may contain **formaldehyde**, a powerful skin irritant, allergen and suspected human carcinogen. The anti-dandruff shampoos may contain **selenium sulphide**, which is also irritant and a carcinogen in animals. This compound may be absorbed through your skin so do not use it in the bath.

Other personal care products

Hazardous chemicals may be encountered in other products too. Bath foamers, for example, may contain formaldehyde. In the average household the bathroom is the place where aerosol cans are most likely to be encountered: see under 'Packaging' (page 39) for more about these. **Acetone** is used in nail varnish and remover and is an inflammable and irritant chemical. Cheap imported cosmetics may be a source of higher concentrations of some of these toxic materials than would be allowed here; some may even contain mercury or lead pigments.

On the positive side, shops and mail-order firms specialising in non-animal products and natural ingredients are becoming ever more popular. While the use of natural ingredients by itself does not guarantee a non-hazardous product, some of these firms (such as the Body Shop chain) will state all the ingredients they use, and staff should be able to tell you if any are known to be allergenic.

Toilet paper and tissues

If we are trying to reduce our personal pollution impact then the toilet roll is something of a problem. Because the dyes are mostly part synthetic and non-biodegradable the use of dyed paper products might seem best avoided. In Sweden however white toilet rolls, tampons and nappies are banned because the bleaching process uses chlorinated compounds and the waste water from paper mills contains **PCBs** and **dioxins**. These are certain to be a much greater pollution threat than the dyes would ever be. There is also a risk from contamination of paper products with dioxins. Some pink paper products are claimed to use a biodegradable dye, so these, or undyed products, are probably the best answer, but the products are not as yet labelled to state what kind of dye they contain.

FOOD AND WATER

Lead on vegetables

The main source of lead in the environment is from leaded petrol fumes, and this lead can be deposited from the air onto soils and crops at considerable distances from roads. Gardens and allotments near roads are however the ones most at risk. Most lead that contaminates vegetable crops has been deposited from the air (rather than taken up from the soil), so the longer a crop has been standing and the leafier it is the more lead it is likely to have. The bulk of this lead will be on the outer leaves, and discarding these and thoroughly washing the remainder of the crop will therefore remove most of the danger. In a few more open types of plant, such as lettuces, air may circulate throughout and the whole plant may be contaminated. Your local environmental health department should be able to analyse some samples of food if you are worried about crops near a busy road. The main threat to health from low levels of lead in the atmosphere is to the mental development of children, so it is important to

protect young children and pregnant women from too much
exposure.

Pesticide residues in food

In 1985, a national survey was carried out by Friends of the
Earth on the public's views on pesticide residues in food. This
showed that 91 per cent of respondents would buy pesticide-free
food if they could, and 86 per cent would be willing to pay more
for it. People are obviously suspicious of the quality of food on
offer today: are these fears well-founded, and what can be done
to minimise the risks?

Up until 1988, there was no statutory system for limiting
pesticide residues on food. The government's belated decision to
introduce legislation came about only when it was required by
EEC law: the result was the Food and Environment Protection
Act.

There is considerable room for doubt as to whether or not the
new laws are good enough, at least in the way they are being
applied. Giving evidence to a committee of MPs in 1986 a senior
Ministry of Agriculture official admitted that the safety studies
on older pesticides may have 'considerable deficiencies in data'.
Safety reviews are planned, but it could take up to twenty years
to do this for all 300 pesticides presently licensed for use. In the
meantime these pesticides will continue to be sold and used on
a routine basis.

In April 1988 the government announced its intention to set
statutory 'maximum residue limits' (MRLs) for the 'most important' fruit and vegetable items in the national diet. A weighty
document was produced listing all the combinations of crops and
chemicals for which MRLs were proposed. Yet when the final
version of this appeared later in the year, some of the proposed
limits had unaccountably disappeared! This must certainly raise
the suspicion that commercial interests are being allowed to hold
sway over the protection of the consumer.

The missing items included one very commonly used chemical,
tecnazene, which is applied to potatoes to prevent them from
sprouting in store. At least one supermarket chain, Marks &
Spencer, clearly feels dissatisfied with the government's action
and has set its own limit for tecnazene on potatoes (the one

recommended by the Codex Alimentarius Commission of the United Nations).

Another of the 'missing' limits was for **dimethoate**, used on lettuces. Dimethoate is an **organophosphorus** insecticide, which is a mutagen and both carcinogenic and teratogenic in animal tests.

There are many ways in which unacceptably high pesticide residues could contaminate the food we eat. Instructions for the use of the chemicals may be misunderstood or ignored. The 'harvest interval' — the time that must pass between the last treatment with a particular chemical and the eventual harvest of the crop — may not be observed. Food in storage may be treated with excessive quantities of fungicides or insecticides: a government scientific committee has expressed disquiet about the crude 'bucket and shovel' methods being used to treat stored foods.

There is also the thorny problem of residues on imported foods. Pesticides, including several that are not cleared for use here, are often used under very poorly controlled conditions in Third World countries; indeed Oxfam estimate that pesticides are responsible for upwards of 10,000 deaths a year in the Third World. In what has been called the 'circle of poison', cash crops with high levels of residues may then be imported and form part of our diet.

Very few samples of food, either home-grown or imported, are routinely tested for pesticide contamination. While the general picture that emerges from testing is that residues are very unlikely to exceed the MRLs, there are disconcertingly large holes in the safety net. Routine sampling usually involves testing for only ten to twenty pesticides, a fairly poor coverage out of over 300!

Some types of produce are more likely to present a problem than others: examples are out-of-season fruit and vegetables, such as strawberries and lettuce, and the 'baby' vegetables such as carrots and beets which are grown in impregnated peat blocks. To minimise your own exposure to chemical residues it is a sensible precaution to avoid this sort of produce. Other steps you can take include thoroughly washing all fruit and vegetables before eating or cooking, but this may be of limited value because some pesticides can penetrate some way into the food itself. Some are also applied in the form of a waxy coating (the fungicide

2-phenyl phenol on lemons for instance) that is very difficult to remove by washing.

With pesticides on food, as with many other contentious uses of chemicals, it is a question of weighing up the risks and the benefits. In a lot of cases pesticide treatment turns out to be mainly a cosmetic measure. The retailers (particularly the big supermarket chains) feel that we will be more likely to buy apples if they are a uniform flawless shiny green than if they had blemishes on. They are probably right too, but as more shoppers become aware of just how that flawless appearance is produced perhaps the supermarkets will find consumer preference changing.

Using organically grown produce is the only sure way to avoid pesticide residues, but this is difficult to find and often considerably more expensive. This situation will improve with time, and asking for organic produce is one of the best things you can do to hurry the process along. You might also write and ask your local supermarket's head office if they have a policy on pesticide residues on food and if they do any of their own testing. Perhaps if all food that had been treated with chemicals was labelled as such it would do wonders for increasing the demand for organic produce!

Drinking water
The chemical contamination of our drinking water supplies is an increasing source of concern to many people. This is a subject of bewildering complexity: many claims and counter-claims are made, the laws relating to water quality are in a state of flux and in many areas are regularly breached. People are in danger of being sold devices to 'improve' their domestic water supplies that may actually make them worse!

The main contaminants that are of concern, and their sources, are as follows:

aluminium, is added in water treatment plants to make the water clearer, and possibly increases in the environment as a result of acid rain;

lead enters water from old pipes and solder;

nitrates come from fertiliser use and other farming practices;

solvents are mainly from industrial use as degreasers etc;

pesticides come from farming and from herbicide use by local authorities etc.

Some other compounds, such as **polycyclic aromatic hydrocarbons** (PAHs), may leach out of pipes lined with coal tar pitch.

Except for the solvents, limits exist for all these contaminants under EEC law. Most of the time drinking water supplies comply with the law, as Water Authorities and supply companies blend water from different sources to keep them within the limits. There may however be times when this is not enough to achieve compliance. You can write to your water supplier and ask about breaches of the limits; Friends of the Earth can give you the precise instructions as to how to go about this.

Part of the problem is with surface water contamination, but the more worrying trend is the increasing threat to the underground aquifers, which supply much of Britain's drinking water, especially in the south and east. Nitrates and solvents have both been responsible for contaminating aquifers and there may be many more that are about to become contaminated, but there is little we can do about it. These substances may take decades to filter through to the underground sources and once they have contaminated a supply it stays contaminated for decades more.

Pesticide contamination is caused mostly by the persistent triazine herbicides such as **atrazine** and **simazine**. The toxicity of these compounds is fortunately relatively low, but they still should not be entering drinking water supplies. There may be other pesticide problems that we simply don't know about, because some pesticide analysis techniques are not precise enough to detect these chemicals at levels where they may be a cause for concern or in breach of EEC limits. Something is surely amiss somewhere if toxic chemicals are licensed for widespread release into the environment and yet we cannot even tell what has happened to them subsequently.

Many householders are concerned to lessen their own intake of all these potentially harmful substances. Bottled waters and various 'purifiers' are gaining in popularity, but these may be more harmful in some ways than the water you started off with! A particular threat comes from the activated carbon filters that are fitted into the supply pipe under the sink. These may become breeding grounds for bacteria, and levels of up to 100 times the EEC limit have occurred. Jug filters are safer because you have more control over them and can change the filters as often as you need. They can be effective in reducing lead, some of which enters drinking water in the form of granules, but otherwise they do not remove much except the chlorine taste.

One problem is that there are no standards for water filters in this country. It is true that some devices are being imported that match up to US specifications, but they may be designed to do quite a different job and operate under quite different conditions.

The water supply to many older houses comes through lead pipes. You may therefore be taking in more **lead** than is desirable, especially if you are in a soft water area (lead is more soluble in soft water). Find out from your environmental health department or water authority if you are likely to be at risk in this way. If you do have lead pipes then you should draw off water for several minutes first thing in the morning so that you are not drinking the water that has been standing in the pipes overnight.

The possible health risks from **nitrates** and the steps you can take to reduce them are described in the A–Z section.

In the end it has to be said that the individual is limited in the steps he or she can take to reduce the risks from these unwanted chemical additions to the water supply. It is really a question of tackling the various problems at source.

FURNITURE

Chipboard
This material is frequently used to make furniture, especially the cheaper kinds of shelving and cabinets. Chipboard may release **formaldehyde**, a powerfully irritant gas that is a suspected human carcinogen, into your home. The release of formaldehyde from chipboard can be reduced by coating the furniture with

varnish or paint if necessary. Keep it away from sources of heat and ensure good ventilation in the rooms where chipboard furniture is kept.

Polyurethane foam

This material has been very widely used as a synthetic stuffing for cushions, armchairs etc. Under everyday conditions its toxicity is low, but as soon as there is a fire it becomes potentially lethal. It ignites easily, burns fiercely and emits large quantities of black smoke and very highly toxic fumes of cyanide. A high proportion of deaths in house fires in recent years have been due to poisoning from burning polyurethane foam. Since March 1989 the sale of polyurethane foam-filled furniture has been illegal unless treated with a fire retardant. The treated produce is known as 'combustion-modified high resilient' (CMHR) foam.

Plastic-covered furniture

This is another potentially dangerous feature in house fires if the plastic material is **PVC**. On burning, PVC gives off highly toxic fumes containing **phosgene** and **hydrogen chloride**. Legal requirements to label new furniture with its fire resistance properties apply to plastic coverings as well as to the fillings.

PACKAGING

Aerosols

At the beginning of 1988 about two thirds of all aerosols available in the UK were filled with **chlorofluorocarbons** (CFCs). By March of the same year all the major aerosol filling companies, accounting between them for over 90 per cent of the market, had announced their intention to phase out the use of CFCs in less than two years. This remarkable turnaround is a sign of how rapidly the scientific evidence on the role of CFCs in depleting the ozone layer moved from being just a theory to a near certainty. It is also a clear indication of the great potential of consumer power: mobilised and informed by Friends of the Earth's *Aerosol Connection* booklet, over 100,000 shoppers left the CFC-containing aerosols on the shelves.

Does the move away from CFC propellants mean that aerosols are now an entirely acceptable form of packaging? Emphatically it does not. An aerosol spray does not give you a great deal of control over how much of a possibly hazardous substance you use, nor precisely where it goes. This is a serious risk in some cases and we have drawn attention elsewhere in this book to some of the products whose use in aerosols we find particularly alarming. The windscreen de-icer containing **methanol** — a highly inflammable liquid and a cumulative poison that is toxic by inhalation and skin absorption — is one example. **Sodium hydroxide**, a strongly caustic substance that is intensely painful and may cause serious damage if it gets into the eyes, is another. Added hazards are the highly inflammable nature of the hydro-carbon propellants, the fact that aerosol cans may explode if punctured or exposed to heat, and the disproportionate expense and wastefulness of the packaging compared with the contents. With aerosols, the price of 'convenience' is a high one.

Most manufacturers are now labelling aerosols to say that they do not contain CFCs; treat any that are not labelled with suspicion! In case of any doubt, you may write to Friends of the Earth for a copy of *Aerosol Connection*, which costs £1.

Blown foam packaging

In 1986 one third of the **chlorofluorocarbons** produced in the EEC were used in the manufacture of foam plastics, making this industry second only to aerosols in the use of these dangerous chemicals. Some of these foam products are quite durable and are used in industry, construction, and transport, but packag-ing — egg boxes, meat trays, burger boxes etc. — accounts for a lot of the output too. As the aerosol industry has moved in response to consumer pressure and scientific opinion, so too has the packaging industry, and many manufacturers and packers have announced the substitution of other products for CFC-blown foams. Alternatives include cardboard and foams blown with hydrocarbons or CFC-22 (HCFC-22), a product that is only about one-twentieth as destructive of ozone as the kinds used in aerosols. Given the urgent need to cut the release of all ozone-depleting substances into the atmosphere (effectively a complete phase-out of CFCs is required to stabilise the situation), a switch to the use of CFC-22 on a large scale seems undesirable.

With the exception of packaging materials householders are not very likely to encounter CFC-22. ICI have announced that they will not be supplying it for 'personal care' aerosols because of doubts about its toxicity.

Film wrap
Some film used for food wrapping is made from **PVC**. There is a danger that **plasticisers** or **vinyl chloride** monomer, which are toxic chemicals, may 'migrate' from the packaging into food. There is a particular risk of this if the food is heated while still in the film or if it is an especially fatty food (as the chemicals are more soluble in fat). For these reasons, you should never wrap food in film while it is still warm, nor put film-wrapped food into a microwave. Fatty foods such as cheese or cooked meats should not be kept in film.

An increasing proportion of the food wrapping film on the market is made with **polyethylene**, not PVC. This does not need plasticisers and does not have the toxicity problems associated with PVC.

PESTS IN PERSPECTIVE

Ants
These are dealt with in the garden section, Chapter 4.

Bats
Apart from the fact that some people have a phobic dislike of them, bats do not appear to do any harm. Indeed, in destroying thousands of insects in a single night's feeding they should be considered useful pest controllers rather than pests! Bats are protected in UK law and attempts to kill or dislodge them are illegal.

If you are having roof timbers treated for rot or woodworm and you suspect that you may have bats in residence, contact the Nature Conservancy Council (address given in Chapter 7). Most areas of the country have bat advisers who will visit, attempt to convince you how cuddly your lodgers really are (in which they often succeed), and advise on the timing of treatment and the type of chemical to use. Our substance list tells you which timber treatment chemicals are believed to be safe. The one to avoid is lindane (**HCH**), which is highly toxic to bats.

Cat and dog fleas and lice

A number of highly toxic insecticides have been marketed in various formulations for ridding pets and their bedding of fleas and lice. These include shampoos based on **lindane** or **carbaryl**, flea collars impregnated with **dichlorvos** or **diazinon** and flea sprays that combine **fenitrothion** with dichlorvos. We have serious reservations about the use of any of these chemicals.

Dichlorvos is a potent anti-cholinesterase agent that the World Health Organisation considers to be 'highly hazardous'; it is also a suspected carcinogen. It has been reported to cause very great reductions in the blood cholinesterase level of cats wearing flea collars.

Diazinon is also an anticholinesterase compound that is highly toxic and has suspected reproductive effects. Agricultural users are warned that diazinon is 'harmful to animals' and it is readily asborbed through the skin.

Carbaryl also has anticholinesterase effects and can be absorbed through the skin. It is highly toxic and laboratory tests have shown carcinogenic and reproductive effects in animals. Animal toxicity experiments show that it is particularly potent in its acute effect on dogs.

Lindane is an organochlorine insecticide that is persistent in the bodies of mammals. It too is a suspected carcinogen and has other long-term and reproductive effects. Cats are particularly vulnerable to organochlorine poisoning.

Fenitrothion is toxic to a variety of wildlife, is readily absorbed through the skin, and is not only an anticholinesterase compound itself but also has a synergistic effect, so that it increases the toxicity of other compounds, such as dichlorvos.

The margin of safety when using compounds such as these must be a slender one and there would seem to be a considerable risk to the pet's health, particularly if the instructions for use are misunderstood or ignored. Children may spend a good deal of their time in close proximity to pets too, and the risk to them is another factor to be taken into account.

There are of course less hazardous chemicals available; for the treatment of bedding **methoprene** seems safer than most. There are also herbal shampoos and oils that have a repellent effect (they should not be assumed non-toxic to pets). Regular washing and airing of the bedding, vacuuming of areas where the pet sleeps or lies (disposing of the dust at once inside a tightly sealed bag) and brushing of the pet's coat may be effective enough on their own.

Flies

Slow-release fly killers are resin blocks impregnated with **dichlorvos**. This is a 'highly hazardous' chemical and we feel the use of these products inside the home is best avoided.

Fly-sprays may also contain dichlorvos or other **organophosphorus** compounds such as **fenitrothion** or **pirimiphosmethyl**. The active ingredient will be stated on the can and you can check against the entry in our A–Z section. We would caution against these compounds in general; most are hazardous to a degree (dichlorvos especially so) and some people are especially vulnerable to their effects.

A few aerosols contain **lindane (HCH)** and these should definitely be avoided.

Pyrethroids are frequently used in fly-sprays because of their rapid effect. The available information suggests that they are generally less hazardous, although they vary considerably in their toxicity and some are reported to be allergens or irritants. **Cypermethrin** is carcinogenic in animal tests. In general do not use a fly-spray where food is prepared or eaten and do not remain in a room that you have sprayed. Check the propellant too, and do not use ones with CFCs.

In tests done by the Consumers' Association fly papers performed quite effectively, but the flies did take a long time to die. Ultraviolet electrocutors were the least effective method of all.

Cut down the potential for flies to breed by keeping all dustbins and kitchen waste bins well sealed with tightly fitting lids. As well as a nuisance flies are a health hazard because they may

land on putrefying matter one minute and your food the next.
Keep food covered.

Head and body lice

These are killed by means of shampoos and creams. We may
think of these as medicinal products but they are basically insecticides and use the same chemicals as garden products. There are
three chemicals used: **HCH**, **carbaryl** or **malathion**. All three
have the potential to irritate and be absorbed through the skin,
but HCH would seem to have the most serious risks attached.
Lice have become resistant to it in some areas. Malathion seems
to be the least hazardous of the three, but it is a potential
allergen. Both malathion and carbaryl can reduce blood cholinesterase levels.

Insect repellants

Solutions for applying to exposed skin most commonly contain
diethyl toluamide (DEET), which is highly toxic if swallowed
and may be absorbed through the skin. Very concentrated solutions of DEET are available and these have caused poisoning
in adults and children, even resulting in death. Repellants should
be used sparingly.

Rats and mice

Chemicals that kill rats and mice are called rodenticides. For
many years the first choice was **warfarin**, an anticoagulant that
causes the animals to die through internal bleeding. Warfarin
has its disadvantages: it is highly toxic to humans by swallowing
or inhalation, several doses are needed to kill the pests and rats
in some areas have become resistant to it. In the last 15 years a
'second generation' of anticoagulants has been introduced. These
chemicals — **brodifacoum**, **difenacoum** and **bromadiolone** —
are at least 100 times more toxic to rats than warfarin. Careless
use of any of these may pose hazards to pets and cases of human
poisoning have been recorded. All three act in the same way,
affecting the liver of rats and mice and killing them from a single
dose. The effect is not immediate, however, and it may be up to
three weeks before the animal finally dies. During this time they
can be picked up as prey items by pets or wildlife and so there

is a risk of secondary poisoning. Because the rodents remain active this may happen even if the chemicals are confined to indoor use as recommended. The barn owl, a declining and vulnerable species in Britain, is particularly at risk from these new anticoagulants.

Although brodifacoum is licensed for use by professionals only, difenacoum and bromadiolone are unrestricted, and may be bought and used by householders.

Haemophiliacs are especially vulnerable to anticoagulants and should avoid any contact with them.

Guard against mice and rats by blocking any potential entry holes into the house and storing food securely in containers. One or two mice can be trapped. If you have a recurrent problem then some biological control in the form of a cat may help.

Silverfish
These creatures are frequently found in kitchens and bathrooms. They are quite inoffensive and are not really 'pests' at all. They are however a sign of damp conditions and there is a danger that rot may develop in timbers if such conditions persist. Do not worry about killing the silverfish; concentrate on eliminating the damp!

Wasps
A variety of insecticide sprays is sold for dealing with wasps around the house; these generally use the same chemicals as in fly-sprays (see p. 43) and the same remarks apply. Lindane **(HCH)** is frequently found in wasp-killer products and we advise against the use of this pesticide. If you have a wasps' nest in your house then it is best dealt with by professionals; contact your Environmental Health Department who will usually have the best service to offer or will be able to recommend an approved firm. Commercial pest control firms may not want to tell you what chemical they will be using but there is no good reason for such secrecy and you should insist on your right to know. Some firms may still be using lindane, although **synergised pyrethrum** or **pyrethrins** will do the job just as well and are less toxic and persistent products.

STATIONERY PRODUCTS

For glues and solvents see under DIY (Chapter 5).

TOYS

Lead in paints
It is now illegal to sell toys that use leaded paints, as there is a serious risk of children taking in lead through chewing the toy. British toy manufacturers have been aware of this hazard for a number of years but imported toys with a high lead content in the paint are still occasionally found. Contact your local Trading Standards Officer if you are concerned about a particular kind of toy.

Hobby hazards
Several chemical hazards arise from hobbies such as electronics and model making. Topics such as soldering, paints, solvents, epoxy resins and glues are dealt with in Chapter 5. Remember that a child or a teenager is more vulnerable to a variety of toxic hazards than is an adult. He or she may spend many hours working with hazardous substances and may be less inclined to heed the warnings printed on packets or tins (if indeed adequate warnings are given). You should not allow children to use solvents and glues unsupervised.

4.

GARDEN AND GREENHOUSE

PESTICIDES

Everyone who has a garden or greenhouse knows that at one time or another they will have some problem with pests and diseases, and many of us will turn to the arsenal of chemicals available from garden centres and hardware shops to combat them. The sheer number and variety of chemicals is bewildering: currently over 100 different 'active ingredients' are licensed for use by amateurs, and they are packaged into well over 400 different formulations or mixtures. How many of these chemicals are really necessary? What sort of risks might their use involve for us, our children, our pets and the wildlife of our gardens?

Most of the garden chemicals we are concerned with are one or another type of pesticide (also sometimes called 'biocide'). This term covers all those chemicals that are intended to protect the plants we want to grow by killing or retarding the ones we don't want — the weeds — and by killing or repelling the multitude of insects, fungi, slugs and other pests that lie in wait to devour them.

Pesticides are further classified as follows:

Herbicides — these are weedkillers and growth retardants. Some are contact herbicides, killing only the plants that the chemical itself lands on when you spray or dust. Others are 'translocated', which means that they are transported within the plant. 'Residual' herbicides remain active in the soil, preventing the growth of plants over a longer period of time. Some herbicides are specially formulated to be selective; for example they only affect broad-leaved weeds such as plantains or buttercups while leaving the narrower blades of grasses unharmed. These kinds have found a ready market as lawn treatments.

Insecticides — these kill pests such as ants, wasps, aphids, cabbage root fly, whitefly, etc. Most act on contact, but some are 'systemic', being taken up into the tissues of a plant and then killing the pests that eat it.

Fungicides — these destroy, or prevent the growth of fungus. Club root in cabbages, the 'damping off' of seedlings, chocolate spot on broad beans and rust and black spot on roses are all examples of fungal diseases that are common in gardens and that these chemicals are designed to combat. The older types of fungicide like **copper sulphate** (an ingredient of 'Bordeaux mixture'), act by direct contact with the fungus or the surface where it might try to grow. More recently a number of systemic fungicides have been introduced.

Vertebrate control — for rats, mice and moles.

Miscellaneous products — mostly slug, snail and earthworm killers.

Several chemicals can act in more than one way, e.g. **dichlorophen** is sold both as a fungicide and a herbicide. Many mixtures are also specially formulated so as to kill more than one kind of pest, or else to combine contact and systemic types, or fast-acting with slower, more persistent, pesticides. Sometimes you may not be aware that you are buying a pesticide at all! For example, many products are sold as rooting powders and you might think that these were just hormone products that encouraged your cuttings to strike successfully. Look more closely at the labels, however, and you will find that many contain a fungicide too and some even have a herbicide as well.

How 'safe' are pesticides?

The chemical industry points to the very low number of recorded deaths or illnesses that can be blamed on pesticides as evidence of the safety of their products. As far as Britain goes, this cannot be denied (though the situation is very different in the Third World); but is this really enough? What about the other effects these chemicals are suspected of causing, which may not show up for years, perhaps not until the next generation?

Of the 105 chemicals licensed for garden use in 1988, there

are 35 for which there are published references to one or more long-term health effects: 16 of these are known or suspected carcinogens, 7 are known or suspected teratogens and a further 12 have both of these undesirable properties. In addition, pesticides may have other effects on human health at quite low dosages. Chief among these is that many of them are irritants and can cause skin rashes and inflammation of the eyes or the membranes of the breathing system. Irritant effects have been recorded for 58 of our list of 105. The 'inert' ingredients in which the pesticides are dissolved may be irritants too.

Does all this mean that we are at risk from using such substances in our gardens? Consider first that many of the same ingredients are used on farms, where users are advised to follow quite complex special safety procedures. These can include protective gear such as neoprene gloves, heavy rubber boots, overalls, goggles, face masks and sometimes even full respirators. Other precautions concern the intervals of time which must pass before any treated produce can be harvested, or new crops sown in treated ground, livestock allowed onto sprayed areas, etc. Contrast all this with the situation in your local garden shop, where these same chemicals are distributed to untrained individuals with a freedom that borders on the reckless. Safety advice with garden chemicals can be vague or sometimes positively misleading (see for example the section on wasps, page 67).

Now it is of course true that the farmworkers who have to handle these chemicals are usually working with much larger quantities, and with more concentrated forms, of the product that you are using in your garden (though this is not always the case). Against this, however, the farmworker is usually a fairly healthy adult. The people exposed to garden chemicals will include small children and people whose disabilities or illnesses leave them particularly at risk. So beware the complacent attitude that you are only dealing with 'safe' formulations of a chemical.

Is there any real evidence, though, for widespread harm resulting from the use of garden pesticides? It has to be admitted that there is not a great deal. One study showed that children in households where garden pesticides were used ran six times the risk of contracting leukaemia as compared to those in non-chemical gardens. This is disturbing, though it does fall short of proof that the pesticides were to blame.

Once again, this looks like a case where the 'precautionary' approach makes the most sense. The risks are low compared with those from cigarette smoking for example. Precisely for this reason, however, it is going to be a long time before any harmful effects show up in the statistics so strongly that no-one can argue about them any more. Why do we have to wait until then? Many gardeners manage with only a bare minimum of chemical pest control and some hints are given in this chapter as to how you can join them if you haven't already.

Sadly, the government seems to think that it is the chemical companies that are most in need of protection, and we are a long way from adopting a precautionary attitude when it comes to garden pesticides. Many chemicals remain on sale here that other countries have seen fit to ban from domestic gardens, or in some cases altogether. So again, beware the complacent attitudes you may come across from the staff of garden centres, or maybe from your employer if you work in horticulture or a council parks department, that 'If the government allows it, it must be safe'!

When we come to consider the environmental effects of garden chemicals, the picture is again disturbing. Most slug killers, to take one example, are based on **metaldehyde**, a poisonous chemical that has been responsible for the deaths of numerous pets, hedgehogs, small mammals and garden birds. While slug pellets are one, rather extreme, case, many other pesticides affect the more humble varieties of garden life such as earthworms, beetles and the tiny springtails that help to create leaf mould. Their loss impoverishes your garden too, for you end up with a poorer soil, less for small birds and mammals such as shrews to live on and a reduced population of 'friendly' insects to keep the pests in check. This is particularly the case with those pesticides that persist in the soil.

Some of the more modern pesticides have been designed to reduce these risks; they are not particularly toxic to mammals and often break down into harmless constituents within a few days. This still does not make them completely 'safe' for wildlife, however. Several such chemicals are synthetic variations of the active principle in **pyrethrum**, a powerful and very fast-acting insecticide derived from a chrysanthemum plant. These **pyre-throids**, as they are known, are all very toxic to fish and can harm other water-borne life in quite tiny concentrations. It is therefore essential to keep such chemicals away from ponds or flowing water. Generally these powerful insecticides make no distinctions between their victims; they are as dangerous to bees, for example, as to the pests you are trying to kill. These draw-backs apply equally to **pyrethrum** itself — one of the few insecti-cides that organic growers do use — but pyrethrum does break down very quickly, and so you can avoid harming bees by spray-ing only in the evening.

In the rest of this chapter, we look first of all at some general rules you can follow in order to minimise the use of chemicals in your garden and to ensure that when you do decide to use them you can do so safely. We then take a more detailed look at some of the various pest problems you might encounter and some of the methods, both chemical and non-chemical, that can be used to control them.

INTEGRATED PEST MANAGEMENT

Avoiding the need for garden chemicals

Organic gardening is growing in popularity and many excellent books on the subject are available. Here we shall do no more than outline a few general rules, which apply whether you are going to be strictly organic or not. What we are aiming for is what is rather grandly called 'integrated pest management' (IPM), a system in which the use of chemicals is only a part, and by no means the most important part, of pest control.

Part of the appeal of the instant-solution-in-a-tin that garden pesticides claim to provide is that you do not have to bother to find out what is happening to your plants. They look wrong, you spray something on, and if that doesn't work you spray some-thing else! So a number of formulations are sold with a formidable mix of different chemicals designed to cure everything at once, whether you have it or not. ICI's 'Roseclear', for example, con-tains two different fungicides and an insecticide; Boots' 'Total Lawn Treatment' contains six different herbicides! This can hardly be called judicious use of chemicals. Quite apart from the additional expense and hazard involved, this kind of treatment against a pest problem that does not even exist (or 'insurance spraying' as it is known in big farm circles) is a sure way to increase the risk of resistant strains of the pest evolving, so that when you *do* need to use the chemical it doesn't work any more!

IPM means a more intelligent approach; you want to know what your problem is and what are the natural processes that are likely to help it spread or keep it in check. How can you help the latter and hinder the former?

(a) Crop rotation If the same plants are grown on a piece of ground year after year then the pests continue to build up their numbers. Moving crops around the garden helps keep pests in check. The clubroot fungus of the cabbage family and various pests and diseases of potatoes are examples of pests that can be controlled to an extent by crop rotation.

(b) Encourage your friends As a general rule 'fast is friendly', i.e. fast-moving creatures such as centipedes, wolf spiders, ladybirds and hoverflies are invaluable allies, destroying the plant-eating pests voraciously. Encourage them by being cautious in your use of chemicals, through companion planting, and through the provision of shelter and 'nature areas' for the larger predators such as hedgehogs and birds. Of course not every form of wildlife that you attract to your garden by sympathetic management will be friendly, but in general the richer and more diverse the life of your garden, the better the chance that a natural balance will result and that no one kind of weed or pest will get out of hand.

(c) Keep your plants healthy Again, as a general rule, the more healthy your plants, the better they will be able to resist pests and diseases. This means keeping plants well fed and watered. There is no substitute for a soil rich in humus and organic matter! Beware creating the conditions for pests and diseases to thrive: over-watering, for instance, encourages stem rots and 'damping off' of seedlings. Rusts and moulds spread rapidly, so removal of diseased plants or foliage is essential. Check the seed catalogues for different varieties: some are specially bred for resistance to

certain common diseases and you may find you overcome a problem almost entirely just by changing to a different variety.

(d) Accept some Losses Even the use of the entire chemical stock of your garden centre will not keep your losses down to zero. A certain percentage for the slugs, greenfly and other unwelcome guests is inevitable and you will just have to live with this. It comes down to a question of balance and personal judgement as to where you draw the line. As we saw in the section on pesticide residues on food (Chapter 3), a lot of commercial pesticide use is simply for appearance's sake, and you do not have to be so fanatical about your own produce (or decorative plants, for that matter).

Wise use of garden chemicals
The first question to ask yourself is do you really need to use a chemical at all? Are you sure that your 'pest' really is destructive or creating an intolerable nuisance? Might there be other ways of controlling it that do not involve the use of chemicals?

The next step is to pick the right chemical for the job. Make sure that it is designed to tackle your particular problem and avoid mixtures that add in several other chemicals for the sake of 'convenience', but which are actually unnecessary. Usually you will find that there are several suitable chemicals and this is where you should try to choose the least hazardous. This is not easy, as the manufacturers do not seem in the least interested in supplying this information in an accessible form. This is one of the gaps that this book aims to fill.

All pesticides must have some degree of toxicity, or they would not work at all; you should bear this in mind when working with them. Always keep pesticides — even in diluted forms — off your skin. If you do splash any on yourself then wash it off immediately. Wear appropriate clothing when working with pesticides. This means long trousers and long-sleeved tops, which you change out of when you have finished. Gloves are a good precaution too (essential in some cases), but beware the use of ordinary household rubber gloves. These offer only a very limited protection against some solvent or oil-based products and by giving you a false sense of security could make the situation worse.

You should especially avoid getting any pesticide in your eyes; if you do you should wash them in cold running water for several minutes. If the chemical concerned is one we have listed as an irritant, or if it says so on the packet, then seek medical advice.

Always keep pesticides in their original containers so that you're quite sure you know what it is you're dealing with, how much to dilute it, what to use it on and when, and so on.

Never buy pesticides from anywhere other than a hardware or garden shop. Make sure they say on the packet, 'cleared for use as directed under the government's pesticides safety precaution scheme' or similar wording. Beware especially the bargain unlabelled packets of 'weedkiller' or whatever that might be offered for sale at a country fair, allotment society shed or the like. Discourage people from dealing in nameless or unlicensed chemicals.

Keep all pesticides under lock and key, in a cool dry place. They should not be kept indoors, especially not in places where food is likely to be kept or eaten.

Do not smoke, drink or eat while you're using pesticides. Put them away, change your clothes, and wash your hands and all other areas of exposed skin before you go on to do any of these things.

Only use the pesticide as recommended. Do not mix different kinds, and pay particular attention to any stated harvest intervals (we give some in our A–Z listing section).

Be very careful not to get the pesticide onto the wrong area, especially if you are spraying. In general, do not spray in windy conditions, nor in sunny weather (when there may be a problem with the active ingredient, or the solvent, turning to vapour). As a rule, do not spray herbicides. Keep a separate bucket or watering can for mixing and using pesticides and never dip these into a water tank or stream.

Do not use pesticides near ponds or watercourses. Cover ponds if you are using any chemical that is toxic to fish, such as derris or pyrethrum.

See if there are any products such as 'touchweeders' or 'weed pencils' available for the job if you are going to use a herbicide.

These are far more discriminating ways of applying pesticides and are to be preferred to sprays or powders.

You will see some chemicals in our listing that have a stated period of time before you can allow access for livestock or poultry. The same of course applies to pets and children — your own or other people's — and frankly we wonder why some such chemicals are licensed for garden use at all.

ALPHABETICAL LISTING OF GARDEN PESTS

This section is not intended to be comprehensive; you will not find every garden pest listed here! It is more to give you an idea of the various ways in which chemicals are intended to be used and the range of alternatives available. We have also tried to highlight some of the more significant chemical hazards, be they risks for the user or for the environment. There is a great deal more to be said about 'pests' and their control and we recommend you contact one of the organisations listed in Chapter 7.

Algae
See under Mosskillers etc.

Ants
Ants may be pests if they nest around the roots of vulnerable plants or in a seed bed, or if they are very close to the house and come indoors to forage for food. Otherwise there seems little reason to kill them; it is true that they move aphids from one plant to another, but you will never have an ant-free garden whatever you do! Only the red ants bite, not the black ones.

Pesticides that are, or were, sold specifically as ant-killers are based on the following chemicals, singly or in mixtures: carbaryl, chlordane, diazinon, dichlorvos, fenitrothion, lindane, pyrethrum or pyrethrins, permethrin, phoxim, pirimiphos-methyl, sodium tetraborate, tetramethrin.

Of these, **lindane, chlordane** and **dichlorvos** are chemicals that we definitely recommend you to avoid. Lindane and dichlorvos have already been covered in the household chapter (p. 42). Chlordane is an organochlorine compound. It is a suspected human carcinogen and teratogen, toxic to wildlife and very persistent in the environment. Chlordane was supposedly banned by an EEC directive in 1981, but the UK government evaded the ban by reclassifying it as an 'amenity' product rather than a 'plant protection' product! This absurd situation has at last been rectified and since 1 January 1989 chlordane has been banned for all purposes other than use on sports turf by professionals. It should no longer be available through garden shops.

The other ant killers have varying degrees of hazard attached to them. **Pyrethrum, pyrethrins, tetramethrin** and **sodium tetraborate** are probably the safest. The latter is the old fashioned '**borax**', long used as an ant killer in house and garden. The old remedy was to mix borax 50:50 with sugar, so that the ants would take it back to their nest and the whole nest would be exterminated. Although borax is recommended as a 'safe' pesticide you should bear in mind that it is poisonous: five to ten grams could prove fatal to a child, likewise to a pet. It should therefore be stored under safe conditions, clearly labelled. Make sure that nothing other than the ants will find the saucers of the mix that you lay out. If used outdoors, the borax–sugar mix should be covered with a piece of wood or tile to prevent the rain dissolving it or pets gaining access to it.

If ants are a nuisance merely because they have nested very close to the house, then try the traditional remedy of kettlefuls of boiling water to persuade them to move.

Aphids

It is most unwise to use a powerful general insecticide such as **lindane** or **malathion** against aphids, for in doing this you will also be destroying your most powerful allies, the predatory insects. The most important of these are ladybirds, lacewing flies and hoverflies. The larvae of all of these (and in the case of ladybirds, the adults too) consume huge quantities of aphids and a healthy population of them is one of the best assets a garden can have. Organic gardeners frequently grow flowering plants such as buckwheat, marigold, or various members of the daisy family among the vegetable beds specifically to attract hoverflies. This is one form of what is known as 'companion planting'.

The speed at which aphids multiply does however give them

a head start on the predators and you may well need to use some chemical method from time to time. The least toxic preparation you can use is soft soap, which removes the waxy protective layer from the aphids and leaves them to dry up and die. The soap is available from organic gardening suppliers (see Chapter 7). Soft soap is made from potassium compounds and is not the same as ordinary household soap which uses sodium ones; these can be damaging to plants. Dilute the soft soap and use it in a hand-pumped spray. Search the plants thoroughly, especially on the underside of leaves, and give all the aphids a thorough soaking. You may need to repeat this treatment two or three times over the space of a few days to defeat them.

A stronger measure is to use liquid **pyrethrum**, taking care to avoid a brand that mixes this product with other, less desirable, active ingredients such as **chlordane** or **lindane**, or with a synergist (usually **piperonyl butoxide**). Pyrethrum is quick-acting and breaks down rapidly, so spray in the evening once the bees are asleep and they will be able to visit your flowers safely by morning.

In greenhouses, aphid infestation may be combated by introducing the parasitic insect *Encarsia formosa* once or twice during the growing season. This is commercially available from organic suppliers.

Synthetic chemicals marketed as aphid killers include: captan, dichlorvos, dimethoate, lindane, malathion, pirimicarb, resmethrin, tetramethrin. **Dichlorvos** and **lindane** we have already recommended should be avoided (see Chapter 3).

Captan is actually a fungicide, not an insecticide. It is included in one brand ('Spraydex') of greenfly killer presumably because the sticky 'honeydew' that aphids exude provides an ideal growing medium for various moulds and rusts to get a hold on the plant. Unfortunately, captan is a potential carcinogen, a suspected teratogen, mutagen and irritant, persistent in soil and harmful to aquatic life in very low concentrations. Some fungi have evolved resistance to it. It is banned for garden use in Sweden and banned altogether in Finland and West Germany. We do not feel we can recommend this brand.

Dimethoate is a systemic organophosphorus insecticide, marketed by Boots and Fisons among others as 'Greenfly and

Blackfly Killer'. It is listed by the World Health Organisation as 'moderately hazardous' and is toxic to mammals, fish and bees. The US Environmental Protection Agency consider it to be a mutagen and have restricted its use. They insist that *anyone* using dimethoate, householders included, should wear protective clothing.

Some gardening books, including some organic ones, recommend the use of **nicotine** as an insecticide, and some even include a 'recipe' for making your own from old cigarette ends. We feel this advice is ill-considered. Nicotine is classified by the World Health Organisation as 'highly hazardous', and swallowing as little as 40 mg can be fatal. It is also rapidly absorbed through the skin. The DIY recipe is particularly dangerous, since you will be splashing around a solution of unknown strength.

Bees
Bees are not pests; they are immensely beneficial insects and the annual value of their services in pollinating crops has been estimated by the Ministry of Agriculture at several million pounds. Recent moves to have bees declared as pests are pernicious and should be strongly resisted.

Having said that, you probably wouldn't want a wild swarm in your roof! If this should happen it is a job for experts to collect the swarm live. Contact your local Environmental Health Department, or look up 'beekeepers' in the Yellow Pages. Do not contact a pest control firm as they will not have the relevant expertise.

Birds
Many species of bird are of course beneficial to the garden: song thrushes eat snails, robins hunt out soil pests, and so on. These are very good reasons why you should avoid the use of slug poisons based on **metaldehyde**; even if you cover the pellets so as not to harm pets, secondary poisoning of thrushes, hedgehogs, etc. that eat the metaldehyde-laced slugs is potentially a major problem. We have very little idea on what scale such poisoning occurs. There are bird enemies too, of course, such as bullfinches and pigeons. There are no appropriate chemical remedies and

protecting plants with netting or cages is the best answer. Model snakes are reported to work well too!

Blights

The traditional remedy for potato and tomato blights, still recommended by some organic gardening authors, is to spray with copper compounds such as **copper sulphate**, usually mixed with calcium hydroxide and sold as 'Bordeaux mixture'. Copper sulphate is moderately toxic if swallowed, an irritant, and possibly an animal carcinogen and mutagen. It is also very persistent in the soil and repeated use on the same patch of ground has a markedly harmful effect on soil life (e.g. in orchards, where Bordeaux mixture used to be sprayed on trees against a variety of fungi).

Fortunately blight is much rarer now than it used to be, because it is so much more effectively controlled in agriculture by a variety of modern fungicides. On a garden scale, the use of resistant varieties helps to insure against blight.

Cabbage root fly

These insects lay their eggs in the soil around the base of the plants and on hatching the larvae (grubs) burrow down to attack the roots of the crop. A simple defence is to lay a square of roofing felt, carpet underlay, or thick card around the base of each plant to prevent the adult from laying there.

Chemical treatments on the market include ones based on bromophos, chlorpyrifos, diazinon, dimethoate and lindane — often as mixtures containing several of these.

We recommend that you avoid lindane. All the others are **organophosphorus compounds**. **Diazinon** and **dimethoate** are both listed by the World Health Organisation as 'moderately hazardous' and are reported to have teratogenic and mutagenic properties. They are also persistent and toxic to mammals and aquatic life.

Carrot fly

This is another pest that lays eggs on the soil and most chemical remedies are based on persistent **organophosphorus compounds**, as for the cabbage root fly.

A recently discovered technique for the protection of a carrot bed is to put a polythene barrier, 75 cm high, all around it. Apparently when looking for disturbed soil in which to lay their eggs the flies travel only a few inches above the ground, so the barrier will keep them away. This method is reported to be very effective. Ordinary polythene is prone to tear so a reinforced kind, or a very fine mesh material such as 'Papronet' is better for this purpose.

Caterpillars

The worst caterpillars in the vegetable garden are those of the two cabbage white butterflies, the large and small whites. A fine nylon net (mesh 1 cm or less) draped over the plants in the summer months is one form of protection. It prevents the butterflies getting onto the cabbages to lay eggs.

There is one biological insecticide on the market that is effective against many caterpillars. This is *Bacillus thuringiensis*, a bacterium that invades the body of the caterpillar and destroys it. It is a mild irritant on the skin or by inhalation, but apart from this no adverse health or environmental effects have so far been reported from its use.

Centipedes and millipedes

Centipedes are the flattened reddish-brown creatures that hide by day in dark and damp places. They are predators and hence useful to the gardener. Don't confuse them with millipedes, which are smaller, rounder, have many more legs and are black or yellowish-brown. Millipedes can be troublesome, eating into potato tubers or other underground parts of plants. Millipedes may be partially controlled by trapping, using perforated containers sunk into the ground and filled with potato peelings as bait. General soil biocides such as **bromophos** or **dimethoate** kill predators just as effectively as they do millipedes, and are also toxic to birds, bees and animals.

Clubroot

This is a serious fungal disease that affects cabbages and all other members of the Brassica family, including radishes and swedes. The best prevention is to keep these crops together and move them around the vegetable plot on a four-year rotation. The common garden weed shepherd's purse is also affected and should be removed whenever it is seen. The fungus does not tolerate lime, so this can be added to the soil before the cabbage bed is moved there.

The control of clubroot is one of only four permitted uses of the toxic mercury compound **calomel**, which we recommend should be avoided.

Cutworms

Cutworms are the larvae of the Yellow Underwing Moth; they live in the surface layers of soil and can be destructive pests of seedlings and tender plants. General soil insecticides such as **bromophos** and **dimethoate** are moderately persistent in the soil — they have to be to do the job — and have the disadvantage of killing predatory insects as well as pests. They are also harmful to bees, birds and animals.

Plants can be protected from cutworms by surrounding them with a collar cut from a clear plastic drink bottle.

Earwigs

Several insecticides, including the persistent and hazardous **lindane**, are advertised as killing earwigs. These insects, however, do very little damage and are really quite inoffensive; their pincers may look fierce but are not strong enough to pierce the skin. Earwigs may be trapped (e.g. for removal from a greenhouse) in sacking or upturned flowerpots filled with shredded paper or straw.

Fruit tree pests and diseases

Correct pruning and the removal of diseased parts are important in keeping fruit trees or bushes in good health. For trees, a 'winter wash' based on **tar oils** is widely used as a general insecticide. Once again the problem with winter washes is that they kill useful insects as well as pests, and indeed have actually created a new pest problem by depriving red spider mites of mosses and lichens on which to feed — so they attack buds and leaves instead! Winter washes are toxic to humans too; tar oils are quite strongly irritant and all tar products are carcinogens.

Grease bands are effective against several insect pests. They contain no chemical insecticide; the traffic of insects up and down the trunk simply gets stuck.

Grease bands do not control the codling moth, however, which is one of the main causes of maggoty apples. A very effective modern remedy is a particularly cunning piece of biological control known as a pheromone trap. The female moths attract males by means of a powerful scent stimulant — the pheromone — and now that this has been chemically synthesised you can buy simple ready-made traps to hang up in the trees at the appropriate season. All the male moths fly to these and become stuck, leaving the females frustrated and your apples whole!

Wounds from pruning or broken branches allow the entry of disease. Traditionally these have been painted with a **bitumen** compound. A recent innovation is to 'inoculate' the wound with a harmless fungus such as *Trichoderma viride*, marketed as Binab. This is also reputed to be effective against other fungal problems such as silver leaf disease, honey fungus and even dutch elm disease. We have no information on the toxicology of *Trichoderma* powder, but it would be wise to treat it as an irritant and avoid inhalation.

Lawn treatments

Some of the most hazardous chemicals that are cleared for use by gardeners are sold for use on lawns, which considering that they may occupy a large area of the garden and that children and pets may roll around on them for hours on end, seems rather strange. These chemicals include **carbaryl**, **chlordane** and **2,4-D** (or at least they did until very recently: chlordane has now been withdrawn from sale to all except professional users). It may also seem strange that the 'pests' that the lawn treatment chemicals are aimed at include earthworms, moss and daisies!

The use of a good quality seed or turf in the first place, then proper use of the mower, lawn rake and besom, should be enough to maintain a lawn in good condition. On anything except a bowling or putting green there is no need to 'control' earthworms; casts may be brushed off and the worms do a valuable job in keeping the lawn aerated and well drained. Leatherjackets can be brought to the surface of the lawn by saturating it then covering the ground with plastic for one or two hours, after which they may be picked up and put on the bird table. Raking and good drainage should keep down the moss; if it becomes too rampant then a **ferrous sulphate** mosskiller could be used. This is harmful to aquatic life, however, so should be used sparingly and not near ponds or watercourses.

Under EEC law, **calomel** may still be used on lawns for the control of dollar spot and *Fusarium*, but it is a persistent and toxic chemical and we do not feel it should be used in domestic gardens.

There are many selective herbicides on the market for control of broad-leaved weeds in lawns. Some of these are included in lawn fertilisers; take care to read the label and see what you are buying. The products on sale usually contain a mix of chemicals: we have already mentioned Boots' 'Total Lawn Treatment', which has six different ingredients. The safety of several of these ingredients is questionable even in isolation, and the properties of mixtures are seldom studied adequately. The irritant potential of **dicamba**, for instance, is reported to be worsened by the addition of **mecoprop**; five garden products, two of them lawn treatments, combine these two chemicals. The most controversial of the selective weedkillers are the chlorophenoxy acids, a group which includes **dichlorprop, mecoprop, MCPA** and **2,4-D**. All have some irritant properties, which may be worse when they are combined. MCPA and 2,4-D are possible human carcinogens. There is evidence to show that 2,4-D has caused a rare form of cancer in farmworkers in the United States. It is banned or restricted in some countries and several local authorities in Britain have now discontinued its use.

Ioxynil used also to be an ingredient of some lawn treatments. It is no longer cleared for garden use, but old stocks may still be found on the shelves of garden shops. If you find ioxynil on sale, point out to the shop manager that these products are now illegal.

Lichens
See next section.

Mosskillers etc.

For moss on lawns, see under Lawn treatments. Stronger mosskillers, for use on paths or drives, may contain **chloroxuron**, which is reported to be slightly toxic to birds and is therefore best avoided.

Some slimy green growths on shaded paths are not moss at all, but algae. Such growth may be hazardous as it can be extremely slippery. Various sterilising washes based on **quaternary ammonium compounds** are available, or a **bleach** solution may be used to remove it.

The same washes are also advertised as effective against lichen growths. Lichens are a fascinating group of plants which have become sadly rare in many parts of Britain because of air pollution; we know of no harmful effects of lichen growth and can think of no reason for killing them.

Some 'patio cleaners' are based on **hydrochloric acid**, a corrosive chemical which should be handled with extreme caution — see the DIY section.

Rooting powders

Several brands of rooting powders (e.g. Sorex, Corry's and Murphy) contain the fungicide **captan**. Captan is a skin irritant and sensitiser and also a suspected carcinogen and teratogen. The chemical has been withdrawn from use in Finland and severely restricted in Norway and Sweden (including a ban on garden use in the latter country). So long as you prevent them from getting too damp, cuttings do not really need a fungicide to take root successfully.

Weedkillers

For selective weedkillers, see under Lawn treatments. Chemical weedkillers for land clearance and for keeping paths and other such areas clear have been around for many years. One of the first chemicals to be used for this purpose was **sodium chlorate**; this is an irritant and very toxic if swallowed. It is also a fire risk: if splashes of the solution dry out on clothing or paper, these will become highly inflammable.

More recently introduced 'total weedkillers' include **aminotri-**

azole, **paraquat** and the triazine herbicides such as **atrazine** and **simazine**.

Paraquat has caused a great many deaths because it is extremely toxic if swallowed — one swallow of a 40 per cent solution is enough to kill an adult — and there is no known antidote. It is also harmful to animals, and is persistent. Once it reaches the soil paraquat is rapidly absorbed onto clay particles and it is assumed that this 'deactivates' it completely. There is however no guarantee that it will stay deactivated for all time (once the clay particles are washed into watercourses for example), nor that it will not contaminate water eventually if it is used on sandy soils. It was this uncertainty about the fate of paraquat in the environment that led to its being restricted in West Germany in 1984.

The **triazine herbicides** are very widely used by local authorities and others to keep pavements, road edges, etc. free from weeds. These chemicals are very persistent and are now starting to contaminate water supplies in many parts of England. Although their toxicity is fairly low, concern about their persistence has led to the inclusion of **atrazine** and **simazine** in the government's draft 'red list' of dangerous chemicals and it seems likely that they will be severely restricted at some future date. Some people may have a strong allergic reaction to atrazine.

If you do need to use a strong weedkiller in the garden, for shrubs such as buddleia or elder that grow in awkward corners, or to clear very deep-rooted plants such as comfrey or horseradish, then the best chemical to use is probably **ammonium sulphamate** ('Amcide'); it should be handled and stored with care, being an irritant and moderately toxic if swallowed. Its main advantage over other herbicides is that it has no known long-term hazards and quickly degrades into ammonium sulphate, a fertiliser.

Glyphosate ('Roundup') has been used increasingly in recent years and is seen by some as a 'safe' herbicide; some nature trusts use it on reserves as it is not persistent and not known to be harmful to wildlife (except to fish). It is however a powerful eye irritant and a skin irritant.

Non-chemical methods are always worth considering first. To break in an abandoned weed-strewn allotment, for example, a good labour-saving method is to cover the ground completely with several layers of cardboard or black polythene, or an old carpet. Strongly growing vegetables can be planted in holes punched through this layer, which otherwise should be left intact throughout the first season to starve the weeds of light. Forest bark mulch can be used around and between shrubs to smother weeds.

Slugs

Slugs have driven many a gardener to despair, and that includes ones who have sprinkled **metaldehyde** pellets around for years. We have already referred to the hazardous nature of this chemical in the section on birds.

Another chemical sold as a slug killer ('Slug Guard') is **methiocarb**, a highly toxic carbamate compound, classified as 'moderately hazardous' by the World Health Organisation. The Ministry of Agriculture advise that this chemical forms toxic substances when broken down and can be dangerous to animals.

Two considerably less hazardous chemicals, sold as slug killers by Fertosan and Septico, are **aluminium sulphate** and **aluminium ammonium sulphate**. Both are toxic or irritant if inhaled or swallowed, but otherwise there seems to be little danger attached to their use. They do not affect earthworms, nor leave toxic residues in slugs. As their effect on the soil is not dissimilar to a prolonged bout of acid rain, they should be used in moderation!

The problem of a slug-infested garden will not be cured by chemicals alone and you will probably need to resort to picking them off plants by torchlight, scattering barriers of crushed eggshells and pine needles round vulnerable plants, setting out 'slug pubs' — shallow saucers of beer slops, water and sugar — and all sorts of equally useless pastimes. The slug is one of nature's survivors.

Soil pests

See the sections on Cutworms and Centipedes and millipedes.

Wasps

Wasps' nests should really only be destroyed as a last resort, for wasps on balance do a lot of good in the number of household and garden pests they kill. They will only sting if you get too close to the nest. If you decide you do have to destroy a nest, then the chemical insecticides sold for the purpose include carbaryl, lindane and rotenone (also known as **derris**).

Because it is a plant product and has been in use for very many years, there is perhaps a tendency to regard **derris** as 'safe': a tendency that one chemical company at least is only too willing to reinforce by marketing it as 'Back to Nature Insect Spray'! In fact **rotenone** (the active chemical ingredient in derris) is classified by the World Health Organisation as a 'moderately hazardous' compound; it is very toxic if swallowed and an irritant that is known to have caused mild skin rashes in people who use it. Several long-term toxicity effects are known in animals, including suspected carcinogenicity. It is also highly toxic to fish.

Rotenone, however, seems preferable to either **carbaryl** or **lindane**, which have toxic hazards at least as great and cause many more environmental problems. Carbaryl is thought to be one of the pesticides most responsible for bee deaths.

Wasps may become a nuisance around the house or garden towards the end of summer and this is a difficult problem to solve. The choice would seem to be between spraying 'knock-down' insecticides based on pyrethrins or pyrethroids (such as **allethrin, permethrin, phenothrin, tetramethrin**) of uncertain toxicity, or leaving sprinklings of the persistent **lindane** around dustbins, refuse heaps, window-sills, etc. This latter plan of action is actually the advice printed on some containers of lindane dust, though it is not one we would recommend. (The same containers advise 'keep away from children', though how you are supposed to do this when you have just sprinkled it all around the outside of your house they don't say.) At least with wasps you know just what the risks are!

Woodlice

The staple diet of woodlice is rotting wood and they seldom do any damage to plants (you may find them in holes in potatoes or other tubers, but they probably didn't make the holes in the first place). The only situation where woodlice are likely to be troublesome is in a greenhouse, and the solution is to keep the greenhouse clean and in good repair, removing broken or rotting wood.

CHEMICAL FERTILISERS

Plants must be kept supplied with nutrients if they are to grow successfully. The most important of these are nitrogen and phosphorus. On most farms these are supplied in the form of chemical fertilisers: ammonium compounds, nitrates and phosphates. Modern chemical-intensive farming is the cause of increasing environmental problems, of which the pollution of water by **nitrates** is just one.

This argument against over-reliance on chemical fertilisers does not really apply on a garden scale; the quantities involved are so small that gardens are an insignificant source of nitrate pollution. Fertilisers do, however, have certain other disadvantages: they suppress the soil-dwelling bacteria that naturally gather ('fix') nitrogen from the air, damage the structure of the soil and are considered by organic growers to promote a lush sappy growth of plants that actually leaves them more vulnerable to attack by insect and fungal pests. So once you start using chemicals you may be forced into an ever greater reliance on them to compensate for the ecological imbalance you have created, and you are on the 'chemical treadmill'.

There are chemical hazards associated with fertilisers; they are a fire risk and may give off toxic fumes when burnt or heated.

Alternatives to chemical fertilisers include compost, manure, green manures and leguminous plants such as peas, beans, clovers and lupins, whose roots are colonised by the nitrogen-fixing bacteria. Consult the gardening books for details.

BONFIRES

All organic garden wastes, except the very woodiest material, should normally be composted and the nutrients they contain returned to the soil. Most kinds of kitchen waste should also be composted. There is no need to burn autumn leaves; small quantities should be added to the compost heap and if you have several trees in your garden then it is worth making a separate leafmould heap. This takes longer to break down than compost but the result is a dark material, very rich in humus, that is ideal for potting compost mixtures, and it's free! Very few bonfires are thus actually necessary: only for woody prunings and occasionally for diseased parts of plants.

Wood smoke, especially from a damp and slow-burning fire, contains a cocktail of chemical pollutants. This may include substantial amounts of **carbon monoxide**, irritant gases and carcinogenic compounds such as benzopyrenes. These are the main cancer-inducing agents in cigarette smoke, and concentrations in bonfire smoke may be hundreds of times higher than from cigarettes. So keep your bonfires to a minimum and burn only dry woody material. Do not light bonfires on still evenings or on misty autumn days when the smoke will hang around for hours.

Another habit that should most definitely be avoided is the burning of plastics on bonfires. **PVC** in particular can give off a variety of highly toxic fumes when burnt, including **phosgene** and **dioxins**. There may be a similar danger from burning old wood that has been treated with timber preservatives. If the preservative in question is **pentachlorophenol** (PCP), then this too can create dioxins and other toxic compounds when burnt. This seems likely to be an increasingly hazardous feature of demolition site bonfires and one that no-one seems to have thought of in using PCP so liberally in building timbers over the past few years.

Old painted wood should not go on bonfires either, as the paint may contain **lead** and the heat of the bonfire is sufficient to vaporise this.

5.

DO-IT-YOURSELF AND CONTRACTORS

The local DIY shop is one of the most comprehensive sources of hazardous materials available without a prescription or special licence. Toxic, corrosive and inflammable substances can be purchased by people without any training whatsoever with no questions asked and, frequently, little in the way of advice concerning their safe use. Indeed in one survey of DIY shops selling lead-containing paints the advice given was generally incorrect and sometimes dangerous.

Of course, not all the materials on sale to the home decorator are hazardous, but the assumption is that because the material is on unrestricted sale it is safe. In some cases one of a material's hazards is generally known but another is not appreciated — white spirit, for instance, is generally recognised as inflammable but how many people realise that it is harmful by inhalation?

The labelling on such products is not always helpful. Larger packages of certain specified substances are required to carry safety warnings by law but this does not apply to small containers nor to mixtures of several materials. Where labels do provide adequate information they are often printed in very small type, are partly obscured by price stickers and may be rendered illegible by drips and spills of the product.

DIY and car maintenance products are listed alphabetically below. If you cannot find a material you are interested in, look in the A–Z section as some substances — e.g. white spirit — are listed there.

ALPHABETICAL LISTING

Abrasives
Abrasives are materials used to rub down and smooth rough surfaces, e.g. before painting. Common examples include sand-paper and wet-and-dry paper, which consist of particles of a hard

material such as grit or powdered glass held on the paper by an adhesive. Traditionally these have been used by hand but there is now a wide range of power tools which make sanding and rubbing down easier. Wire (steel) wool is another common abrasive used on woodwork.

The abrasive materials themselves are not hazardous in normal use, although in industry abrasive dusts can be harmful and wire wool can leave tiny fragments of metal in the skin which can be irritating. The dust produced when they are used on certain surfaces, however, may be very hazardous. Any paint applied before the Second World War (apart from emulsions and distemper) may have very high levels of lead in it and serious poisoning has resulted from the careless rubbing-down of such paint. Even as late as 1987 paints containing some added lead were on sale, although levels were much lower than in the pre-war products. Because of this, wood and metal paints should not be rubbed down dry: the use of wet sandpaper prevents the escape of toxic dust. Be sure to dispose of the waste carefully and keep children and pets away until the affected area has been cleaned. Wood dusts are irritants and some, especially certain hardwoods, are thought to be carcinogenic. Wear a dust mask when sanding large areas, especially when using power tools. Eye protection is also advisable when power sanding. Never rub down asbestos or lead pipework.

Adhesives
There are many different types of adhesive available for use in the home but from the point of view of safety they can be divided into a few basic groups. Cement-based adhesives are often used for ceramic tiles and these do not present a risk to health apart from the possibility of skin irritation from the cement and from the fungicides that are sometimes included in the mixture.

A wide range of organic solvent based materials is available for sticking wood, cork, tiles, carpets, fabrics and other materials. The two main risks here are of fire and solvent poisoning. The solvents used are normally inflammable, so do not smoke while using such products. Ensure that there are no naked flames in the room — watch out for the pilot lights of gas appliances. Smoking is obviously dangerous when using this type of adhesive because of the fire risk. In addition some products contain **1,1,1-trichloroethane**, which forms toxic **phosgene** when partly burned. Inhaling the solvent vapours can also be dangerous — many adhesives contain toluene, other hydrocarbons and/or chlorinated hydrocarbons. These products are often used by solvent abusers, since the vapours produce intoxication, delirium and sometimes hallucinations. Long-term effects on the heart and liver can be very damaging. An additional risk posed by solvent adhesives is skin irritation — some people may be especially sensitive to these materials.

A common type of adhesive for wood and paper is **PVA (polyvinyl acetate)**. This is of low toxicity and does not normally cause skin problems, although some brands may contain fungicides. Animal and starch glues which are also used for paper tend to be safe, although some people may exhibit allergies.

Some two-part adhesives, based on **epoxy resins**, may pose special risks. The epoxy part may irritate the skin severely and the vapour can be harmful. Such substances are suspected carcinogens. The curing agent, an amine, is also irritant and toxic. Both parts may cause allergies. Once the product is mixed and cured the toxic properties all but disappear, providing that the proportions are correct and there is no unreacted material of either type left.

A comparatively new type of adhesive is the **cyanoacrylate resin**, known as 'superglue'. This has a harmful vapour and poses a special risk since it bonds flesh quickly and very effectively. Use it with care.

The general rule when using any adhesive is keep it off your skin as far as possible, use the product in well-ventilated conditions unless it is water-based and beware of the fire hazard when using solvent-based products.

Antifreeze

Antifreeze consists mainly of **ethylene glycol** diluted with varying proportions of water depending on the brand. The product is toxic if swallowed in moderate quantities and should be kept off the skin to prevent irritation.

Battery acid

Battery acid is a strong solution of **sulphuric acid**. It is highly corrosive and poisonous, causing serious skin burns and damage to clothing. Always wear rubber or strong plastic gloves and eye protection when handling this material, and remove any splashed clothing at once. Wash any splashes from the skin immediately with plenty of cold water and bathe the area in large quantities of a solution of sodium bicarbonate. See a doctor if large areas are affected or the pain persists. Do not add battery acid to any other chemicals and when diluting it add acid to water rather than water to acid. Avoid handling the powdery material which sometimes accumulates around battery terminals — this is toxic.

Brake and clutch fluid

The standard type of brake and clutch fluid is based on **polyalkylene glycol ethers**. These are harmful if swallowed and may irritate the skin with prolonged exposure but are otherwise not particularly hazardous. Other products are based on mineral oils, which may cause skin irritation. Both types are inflammable but not dangerously so.

Brake and clutch linings

Asbestos has long been used in brake and clutch linings, although some manufacturers have now introduced asbestos-free alternatives. When purchasing replacements, check with the manufacturer that they do not contain asbestos. When changing brake linings, do so in the open air and avoid breathing the dust. Wash your hands thoroughly and remove any contaminated clothing before entering the house — wash the clothing immediately. If you cannot get asbestos-free replacements, handle new linings very carefully and clean up any particles that may be rubbed off them. Wrap old linings in plastic before disposal and ensure that children cannot play with them.

Cement

Cement is mixed with sand to produce mortar and with sand and gravel to produce concrete. Tiling grouts are often cement-based as well. It is a dusty material to handle and causes irritation to the eyes and throat. Severe burns can result from prolonged contact with wet cement so wear gloves and protective clothing when handling, mixing or using large quantities of cement products. Use a dust mask when mixing mortar or concrete.

Cement waterproofer

Cement waterproofer is a silicone compound that is mixed into the mortar or concrete before it sets. The concentrated liquid may be irritating to the skin, but treated cement mixes pose no additional hazard as a result of their waterproofer content.

Chipboard

Chipboard consists of particles of wood held together by a resin to give a cheap material for furniture making and other non-structural. Often it is covered with a layer of wood veneer, melamine or other plastic material for decorative purposes, but it may be used in its raw state for flooring. Some chipboards contain resins that emit **formaldehyde**, an irritant and probable carcinogen. It is difficult to avoid chipboard in modern houses, but sealing it with varnish will reduce the rate at which formaldehyde is emitted, as will well-fitting impervious floor coverings on chipboard floors. Ventilation will help to reduce formaldehyde levels in the house. Cutting or sanding chipboard will temporarily increase the rate at which formaldehyde is released, so ensure plenty of ventilation when doing so and wear a dust mask to protect yourself from inhalable dust. Clear up and dispose of sawdust promptly.

Chrome cleaner

Most cleaners and polishes for chrome consist of a mild abrasive in a paste form — the mixture may include a solvent. In some cases the solvent may be harmful — e.g. a petroleum distillate — and some products may contain other ingredients to improve the shine. **Ammonium oxalate**, a toxic material, is sometimes used. Avoid breathing the vapours emitted by these chrome cleaners, do not get excessive quantities on your skin and wash your hands after using them.

Clutch fluid
See Brake and clutch fluid.

Colour restorer
Colour restorer for cars is a mild abrasive used to bring back the colour of paint. Some products include petroleum distillates in the formulation and the vapours should not be inhaled, so do not use them in unventilated spaces. They may cause skin irritation and are inflammable. Colour restorer for use on wood contains a mild acid that should be kept off the skin and out of the eyes.

Damp-proofing fluid
Damp-proofing fluid is injected into brick and stonework just above ground level to form a 'chemical damp course'. The main ingredient is a form of silicone, that prevents the passage of water, but this is dissolved in an organic, usually **hydrocarbon**, solvent. The silicone is harmless in place but the hydrocarbon vapours may be harmful to health as well as inflammable. Exposure to these vapours can cause coughing, irritation and headaches, so ensure that any treated premises are thoroughly ventilated until the smell of the treatment subsides. If you are using these materials yourself, do so in well-ventilated conditions and wear protective clothing, since they can irritate the skin. Do not smoke.

Damp start
Damp-start sprays coat the electrical parts of a car engine with a plastic film that repels water. The plastic material is dissolved in solvents, which evaporate and leave the film behind. It is the solvents that are the most hazardous aspect of the product. **Xylene** and **trichloroethylene** are commonly used. These are inflammable and toxic so do not use these products in enclosed garages and avoid breathing the vapour or spray.

Damp treatments
Many different products are marketed as damp treatments, but they all work on the principle of putting a barrier between the source of water and the inside of the building. The barrier may

be a water-repellent silicone compound absorbed into the brick or stone, as in damp-proofing fluids. With such products the same precautions should be taken as described above, with the added point that you should wear eye protection if brushing the liquid on to the affected surface. Other treatments form a surface membrane of rubbery or plastic material that is then usually painted or wallpapered.

Once dry, these materials are generally non-hazardous, but since they dry in part by the evaporation of solvents, they pose risks while being applied and while drying. Good ventilation is essential, especially if a large area is being treated, and you should avoid splashing the compounds on your skin. This last point is especially important with bitumen-based products, since bitumen presents a cancer risk. Liquid rubber preparations, and the special primer required, contain isocyanates, which can cause serious lung problems in certain individuals. The fluids sold for cleaning up splashes of some damp-proofing products contain solvents such as **toluene** and **xylene**: these are inflammable, harmful by inhalation and should only be used in well-ventilated conditions.

Diesel

Diesel fuel is a mixture of hydrocarbons used mainly in heavier vehicles and construction plant, although some smaller cars are now available with diesel engines. It is less inflammable and less volatile than petrol, although it will burn fiercely when ignited. Diesel fuel does not contain lead and a properly adjusted diesel engine can be quite clean. Badly tuned diesel engines emit large quantities of air pollutants, including smoke and carcinogenic materials. The fuel itself may irritate the skin, the vapour is harmful in large quantities and diesel is a recognised carcinogen.

Dry and wet rot treatments

These products consist of a fungicide dissolved, usually, in a hydrocarbon solvent. The fungicide is intended to kill the organisms responsible for dry rot and some products also contain an insecticide to kill woodworm and other insect pests of timber (see Woodworm killers). The active ingredient may be **pentachlorophenol** (a toxic and possibly carcinogenic organochlorine compound), **tributyltin** (a substance suspected of attacking the immune system) or one of several compounds of copper or zinc. Some new fungicides have been introduced recently, e.g. boresters and carbamate derivatives, and we have limited information as to their toxicity. Some timber is supplied already treated with preservative: the compounds involved are usually a mixture of copper, chromium and arsenic.

Pentachlorophenol and **tributyltin** are probably the most hazardous of the active ingredients available to the general public and these should be avoided where possible. All of these products should be regarded as dangerous and you should always wear impervious gloves, protective clothing and eye protection when using them. Wash splashes from the skin immediately and avoid breathing the solvent fumes, which may be harmful — take frequent fresh air breaks if working in a confined space and ensure good ventilation wherever possible. Keep pets and people out of treated areas until the solvent smell has died down and wash your hands after handling treated timber. The solvent vapour can be ignited by a spark so the electricity supply should be switched off before treatment starts and left off for twenty-four hours. Pilot lights on gas appliances should be extinguished until the solvent smell has died down.

There are alternatives to these products. The first of these is control of moisture. Neither wet nor dry rot can live without moisture, and usually arise when there is rising damp or a leak in the structure of the building. Once the source of moisture has been identified and dealt with, rotted timbers can be replaced (allow a wide margin around dry rot as it spreads invisibly at first) and walls carrying dry rot filaments can be washed down with diluted bleach — some replastering may be necessary. Consult a surveyor if you are uncertain about the spread of dry rot and where the problem has been severe. Timbers vulnerable to wet rot — e.g. window-sills on the rainy side of the house — can be protected with pellets of **disodium octaborate** placed in pre-drilled holes, which are then filled and painted. These will slow the spread of wet rot should the timbers become soaked.

Masonry and brickwork treatments designed to kill dry rot may be based on bleach, as described above, or **sodium *o*-phenyl phenol**, **dodecylamine**, **dichlorophen**, **dichlofluanid**,

quaternary ammonium compounds, **tributyltin** or **pentach-lorophenol**. The last two should be avoided: all are irritants so wear gloves and eye protection when using them. Do not breathe the spray if you are spraying these materials.

Engine cleaner

Engine cleaner is designed to emulsify grease and oil on car engines so that heavy deposits of greasy dirt can be washed away. It contains **cresylic acids** and is very poisonous if swallowed. Wear protective clothing, gloves and boots to prevent skin contact and do not allow the washings to drain into streams or drains running directly into rivers as they are likely to cause pollution.

Filler, acrylic

Acrylic fillers are applied as a paste or semi-solid to gaps and cracks in a variety of situations and set to a fairly hard consistency on exposure to air. They are non-toxic when cured but some people may be sensitive to them, so keep the uncured filler off your skin.

Filler, cellulose

Cellulose fillers are powders that are mixed with water and applied as a paste to fill cracks and small holes in paintwork, plaster etc. They are not toxic in normal use but the dust produced when they are rubbed down may be irritant to the eyes and lungs. Wear a dust mask if you are sanding down large areas of cellulose filler.

Filler, expanding

These products consist of a foam, dispensed from an aerosol can, which hardens to fill gaps and spaces with a rigid material. They contain **isocyanates**, which are toxic and can cause severe irritation of the lungs in sensitive people. If you have to use these products ensure that the room is very well ventilated while the foam is being used and while it is drying. Do not use expanding filler if you suffer from asthma or know you are sensitive to this type of chemical. Keep the material off your hands and out of your eyes.

Filler, exterior
Exterior fillers are usually cement-based, with resins to provide adhesion to the stonework etc. that is being filled. Avoid skin contact when using them, as they may cause irritation. These fillers are not normally rubbed down after being applied, but if you do so wear a dust mask if large areas are involved or if you are using a power tool.

Filler, two-part
Two-part fillers are used to provide a hard and durable filling for woodwork and car bodies. They are generally based on polyester resins and set when the two components are mixed. The resin paste may contain up to 20 per cent **styrene**, which has a toxic vapour, while the hardener is usually **benzoyl peroxide**, an irritant.

  When using two-part fillers you should avoid skin contact with the chemicals and ensure plenty of ventilation. If you rub down the fillers after use, wear a dust mask as the dust may be harmful, and clean up the mess promptly.

Glass fibre
See Mineral wool.

Grease
Grease is a mixture of heavy petroleum compounds used for lubricating machinery and vehicles. It is not particularly hazardous, although it will burn, but it may irritate the skin, especially in people who are sensitive. Old grease containing metal particles may be more hazardous in this respect. Use a barrier cream if you are likely to handle large amounts of grease, and clean your skin with a proprietary cleaner — not petrol, paraffin or white spirit.

Grout
Grouts are used to fill the spaces between tiles and come in two basic types: cement-based and epoxy. They also include colourants, which are generally mineral in nature. Cement-based grouts are irritating to the skin and may cause burns on prolonged extensive contact. Epoxy grouts may also cause skin

inflammation in sensitive people. Both types are harmless when set. Grouts designed for use in wet conditions may also contain fungicides and should be treated with caution as these may irritate the skin.

Insulation, cavity wall

Several different materials are used as cavity wall insulators. They may be placed between the two leaves of the wall as it is being constructed, or injected later. **Polystyrene**, in slab or bead form, is common — this poses no hazards in normal use, although in a fire it will emit toxic fumes. Mineral wool is also used, and this is harmless once installed. Urea–formaldehyde resin, which is injected as a mixture of liquids which then form a foam within the cavity, has caused some problems. As it cures, and for some time afterwards, **formaldehyde** gas is given off and this can reach the interior of the house. Some people are very sensitive to formaldehyde and a range of minor but distressing conditions such as eye irritation and headaches has been linked to the use of this material. Formaldehyde is also suspected of being carcinogenic in humans. We recommend one of the other materials rather than urea–formaldehyde foam.

Knotting

Knotting is a solution of special varnish in alcohol, used for sealing the knots in timber before painting. It is inflammable and excessive inhalation of the vapour can be harmful. It is poisonous if swallowed.

Lacquer

Lacquer is a thin transparent coating used to protect ornamental items such as brassware and art and craft items. One traditional version, shellac, consists of crushed beetles dissolved in ethanol, while others consist of a variety of resins in a solvent such as turpentine. More modern products are based on a plastic material dissolved in solvents such as **ethyl acetate**, **ethanol** and **acetone**. These materials are highly inflammable and the vapours may be harmful, so ensure that you do not use them in a confined space. They may also irritate the skin. Authentic Japan lacquer is poisonous and highly irritating to the skin when wet, but non-hazardous once dry. Some old lacquers contained lead, so wet sand them if you are suspicious or remove them chemically, taking care to clear up the mess thoroughly (see also Varnishes).

Leading (for windows)

Many old windows consist of small panes of glass set into lead strips, and many new ones have lead strips glued to the surface for decorative effect. Also, it is possible to buy lead strips to stick on windows for decoration. This lead can present a hazard if abraded: if clippings and fragments of lead strip are picked up and eaten by children, serious illness could result. To prevent the release of lead dust from existing leaded windows, always clean them gently and wash cleaning cloths out thoroughly. A coat of clear varnish on the surface of the metal will help to prevent abrasion and a matt version would hardly be noticeable. It is best to avoid using decorative lead strip but if you must, make sure that no particles of lead are left behind, ensure that children cannot get access to the materials, wash your hands thoroughly after using it and varnish it after installation. If you wish the lead to darken before varnishing, leave it for a few weeks and do not rub it. Children, particularly those who like to pick at things, should not be allowed to gain access to leaded windows.

Liquefied petroleum gas (LPG)

This term covers several hydrocarbon gases, notably **butane** and **propane**. When used to power motor vehicles the term normally used is LPG, and a mixture is used. Propane (in red containers) and butane (in blue containers) are also used individually in heating and cooking appliances as well as in some DIY equipment such as blowlamps and soldering torches.

These gases are, of course, highly inflammable and are heavier than air, which means that they tend to collect in layers along the ground, especially when cold. They may cause drowsiness and disorientation if inhaled for long periods (some solvent abusers use butane) and high concentrations can lead to suffocation. The incomplete combustion of LPG results in the production of a variety of irritants and the gases can be converted into harmful air pollutants in sunny urban atmospheres. If you use any equipment that runs on LPG check it regularly for leaks and do not breathe the gases when changing cylinders or dealing with leaks. Never smoke when gas is likely to escape or near stored cylinders.

Lubricating oil

Lubricating oil consists of a mixture of heavy hydrocarbons with a variety of additives to modify its properties in engines etc. It is inflammable, but much less easy to ignite than petrol or paraffin. It can irritate the skin. Used engine oil is a dangerous material, since it contains lead and a wide variety of toxic components produced from the burning of fuel in the vehicle engine. Never burn used engine oil and do not pour it down the drain; take it to an approved collection point. Keep it off the skin, as the polycyclic hydrocarbons present cause cancer. A barrier cream can provide useful protection.

Mineral wool

Mineral wool (or man-made mineral fibres) is a general term covering insulation materials made from glass fibre, rock wool and similar material. These are widely used as alternatives to asbestos, which is now regarded as too dangerous to use for routine insulation purposes. Mineral wools can irritate the skin and eyes, although workers using the materials regularly usually get used to them and the symptoms disappear. Coughing and throat irritation also occur in some people.

There is growing concern that these materials may cause similar problems to asbestos, and reliable information on their safety or otherwise is lacking. One study has shown a small increase in the rate of lung cancer in exposed workers, and experts are calling for more investigations.

When using these products you should wear a dust mask and eye protection. Gloves are essential — they should be strong and not knitted, to keep out fibres. Irritated skin can be soothed by running cold water over the affected area — do not rub it as this can make matters worse. If you get the material in your eyes, bathe them gently with cold water and see a doctor if the irritation persists.

Mould treatments

Mould on brick and stone or walls where condensation is a problem can be treated with a variety of chemicals, but if a long-term solution is to be achieved the source of damp must be dealt with, e.g. by repairing leaks or improving ventilation. Bleach (sodium hypochlorite) is used in various dilutions to kill mould; this should be handled with care as it is toxic and irritant. Use gloves, and goggles if brushing it on high or rough surfaces, and do not mix it with other chemicals as poisonous chlorine gas may be produced. More prolonged effects are obtained with other chemicals, e.g. **dodecylamine**, which prevents the re-growth of mould for a while. This, too, is an irritant and should be kept off the skin and out of the eyes. Other fungicides present in mould treatments include **carbendazim** and **quaternary ammonium compounds**, and these should be handled with similar caution.

Paint

Paints provide a protective and decorative coating for a wide variety of surfaces and they generally do this by chemically forming a plastic-like film as they dry. The average tin of paint may contain dozens of ingredients, but the main ones are resins, which form the film, solvents, which keep the paint liquid and enable it to spread, pigments, which give the paint its colour and driers, which promote the chemical processes that form the dried film. Specialist paints have other ingredients — exterior paints may contain cement, textured paints contain fibres or grains of silica, for instance — and many paints dry in part by the evaporation of solvents.

Primers are the first layer of paint to go on a fresh surface; a wide variety is available. They seal the surface, in the case of wood, and help to secure the next layer of paint. They do not normally have much pigment in them and dry fairly quickly. Most primers on sale to the general public are lead-free (the lead driers which were used until recently have now been discontinued), but trade outlets still stock white lead primers. Do not use these paints and ensure that any painters you employ do not use them either. Most primers are oil-based — they do not mix with water and contain organic solvents — but some are quick-drying acrylic products that mix with water. One recently introduced type of primer for exterior woodwork penetrates into the wood and contains three fungicides — **tributyl-tin**, **zinc naphthenate** and a methyl-2-benzimidazole **carbamate** derivative. This should be regarded as a pesticide rather than a paint — wear gloves and use eye protection if appropriate and observe the precautions on the label rigorously.

An unusual hazard sometimes occurs with aluminium primers, which are used in harsh environments, for resinous woods and to overpaint persistent stains. If water enters the tin it can react with the aluminium to produce hydrogen gas, which may build up a high pressure under the lid. Tins of aluminium primer should be opened very cautiously, especially partly used ones, and you should not smoke while doing so as hydrogen forms an explosive mixture with air.

Metal primers help to bond top coats to metal, but their main function is to protect the metal against corrosion. Lead versions, such as **calcium plumbate** and red lead, are still available to the trade and these should not be used. Red oxide, zinc phosphate and zinc chromate primers can be used instead.

Undercoats are designed to improve the covering power of paint systems and have high levels of pigment in them. Some are water-based acrylic types but most are oil-based. They are not leaded.

Top coats are normally glossy, but satin and more matt finishes are becoming popular. They are usually oil-based and may contain additives such as polyurethane for hardness or silicone for extra water protection or glossiness.

Emulsions, or vinyls, are interior water-based paints that dry to a matt or silk finish. They are unleaded and are used mainly for walls and ceilings. Similar in appearance, although with a different chemical composition, are the acrylic interior paints marketed for use in nurseries and on children's toys. These, too, are water-based and lead-free. Water-based acrylic paints are also used for exterior stone and cement work, where they provide decoration and some protection, although painting some types of stone (e.g. Bath stone) can result in greater damage from the weather than if it was left unpainted. Some **exterior paints**, which generally have a rougher texture than the smooth acrylics, are cement-based. **Greenhouse paints** often contain high levels of lead: do not use these but choose an exterior gloss system instead. Some exterior paints, and special 'anti-condensation' paints, contain fungicides or mould inhibitors — treat these with added caution.

Spray paints, as used on cars, are normally based on nitrocellulose and dry mainly by solvent evaporation. The solvent in question is often xylene, and versions suitable for brushing on contain xylene and isobutanol with 2-ethoxyethanol or xylene and ethylene glycol acetate. **Enamel paints**, which dry in a similar manner, also contain xylene, while those that produce a 'hammered' finish contain trichloroethylene as well.

Paint hazards The hazards from using paint are twofold: first, all oil- or solvent-based paints are inflammable, and many can give off sufficient vapour to ignite on contact with a flame or cigarette end if used in enclosed spaces. This does not apply to water-based paints. Second, the solvent vapours may be toxic. In addition, some specialist paints — notably those containing lead — pose particular risks.

As a general rule you should avoid breathing paint fumes as far as possible and work in well-ventilated conditions. Some of the solvents — notably **white spirit**, **xylene** and **trichloroethylene** — are known to be dangerous to health and some can make you drowsy. Spray paints can be particularly risky as the solvents are volatile and evaporate very easily from the spray. Do not smoke when painting since some solvents form more toxic compounds when drawn through a hot cigarette end. A hot surface or flame in the room — e.g. a cooker — can cause the partial combustion of solvents which forms a variety of irritant chemicals as well as being a fire risk. Avoid sleeping or living in recently painted rooms while the paint smell is strong — your nose can be a good guide here! Do not get large amounts of paint on your skin — as well as possibly causing irritation this may result in solvents being absorbed.

When rubbing down old paint for repainting use wetted sandpaper, as old paints can contain dangerously high levels of **lead**. Even modern paints pre-1987 contained more lead than is desirable and children, in particular, should be protected from sanding dust. Do not use power tools for sanding paint as they disperse large amounts of easily breathable dust. Do not use blowlamps to remove old paint either as they vaporise lead, but hot-air strippers can be used providing that they do not operate at a temperature greater than 500°C. Handle stripped paint carefully and dispose of it, well wrapped, in the dustbin. Do not burn old paints, as lead will be released into the atmosphere.

Paintbrush cleaners and restorers

These products contain **organic solvents**, sometimes with a detergent, and are designed to remove paint from recently used brushes. Brush restorers are designed to remove dried paint from brushes so that they may be used again. The solvents in question are usually **naphtha** and other petroleum derivatives, while the more powerful brush restorers contain **dichloromethane** as well. The vapours of both types of products are harmful and they are inflammable. Both may irritate the skin and the products containing dichloromethane are especially powerful irritants. Do not use these materials in badly ventilated places or while smoking and keep them off the skin. Take great care not to get them in your eyes.

Paint strippers

There are two basic types of paint strippers: those which are based on caustic alkalis and those which use organic solvents to dissolve the paint.

The caustic type, which is usually sold as a dry powder to be mixed into a paste but is sometimes available ready mixed, should be handled with great care as it will burn the skin and damage clothing, furnishings etc. Be careful not to inhale the dust when mixing it and clean up any spillage immediately. Wear gloves when mixing the material and eye protection if more than a small amount is involved. Dispose of the waste by wrapping it in plenty of paper and putting it in a plastic bag in the dustbin — it may still be caustic and could also contain large amounts of lead if old paints have been removed. Caustic strippers may damage wood and make it difficult to repaint.

Solvent-based paint strippers contain **dichloromethane**, often with **methanol** as well. Products designed to remove varnish may also contain **trichloroethylene**. These chemicals are all poisonous if swallowed or inhaled and can present a fire risk. Products containing **dichloromethane** are painfully irritating to the skin.

Use these products only in well-ventilated conditions, do not smoke (other toxic chemicals may be formed as the vapours are drawn through the cigarette) and wear gloves which do not dissolve in the product. Use eye protection if you are brushing large amounts, especially on irregular or high surfaces. The gel type is easier to use as it is less mobile. Some types have to be washed off with white spirit, which involves another risk, so water-soluble types are preferable (although the water may damage some woods).

Dispose of the paint waste carefully as described above, as it may be leaded. Wet any newspapers contaminated with white spirit to reduce the risk of fire, and do not pour solvent-based paint strippers down plastic waste pipes as they may dissolve them.

Paraffin

Paraffin is a mixture of hydrocarbons used as a heating fuel. It is less volatile and does not catch fire as easily as petrol, but will burn fiercely once ignited. Its vapour is harmful in excessive quantities and prolonged skin contact may cause dermatitis. It is poisonous if swallowed. Appliances burning paraffin should be used in ventilated conditions, as combustion fumes and condensation may cause hazards to health.

Keep paraffin off the skin and do not breathe large quantities of its vapour. Never use petrol in an appliance designed to use paraffin, as it may explode.

Paste

Wallpaper paste is generally based on cellulose, which is non-toxic. Some modern brands, however, have a PVA adhesive included, and many brands include a fungicide. The risks in using wallpaper paste are very small, but you should not get the material in your eyes or swallow it — children should not be allowed to play with it or use it for modelling etc. Excessive skin contact may cause irritation in sensitive people, but paste is easily washed off.

Patio cleaner
There are three basic types of patio cleaner: those based on detergents, those based on fungicides and those based on **hydrochloric acid**. The first type, like any detergent product, can irritate the skin and should be used with reasonable care to prevent excessive skin contact. Fungicidal patio cleaners, which are usually based on **quaternary ammonium compounds**, may also irritate the skin and should be handled carefully — take special precautions to ensure that the residues do not drain into fish ponds.

The acid type of cleaner should be handled extremely cautiously, as hydrochloric acid can cause severe burns to the skin and gives off a choking vapour. When handling the concentrated product you must use rubber or sturdy plastic gloves and eye protection. Keep a bucket of cold water handy in case of splashes and spillage and if you suffer a burn wash the area with lots of water and a solution of sodium bicarbonate. Do not put the material in a metal bucket. When applying the diluted product wear rough clothes and rubber boots which do not leak. Keep pets and children off the treated area until it has been thoroughly washed down with plenty of water, and clean your boots as well.

Petrol
Petrol consists of a complex blend of organic chemicals, the vast majority of which are hydrocarbons. Additional ingredients include **lead** (except in unleaded fuels) and **dibromoethane**, a carcinogenic material which removes lead particles from the engine when leaded fuel is burnt.

The combustion of petrol, especially in badly tuned engines, produces considerable pollution in urban areas, where the fumes cannot disperse easily. In sunny climates the result can be a very unhealthy smog, while the use of leaded petrol has resulted in elevated lead levels in the environment almost everywhere (see Carbon monoxide, Hydrocarbons, Nitrogen oxides, Ozone).

The inflammability of petrol is well known, yet some people still smoke when filling up their cars. Less widely appreciated is the toxic nature of petrol fumes. The hydrocarbons in petrol include **benzene**, which can cause leukaemia, **toluene** and other toxic materials. Petrol vapour has caused cancer in experimental animals and it may have resulted in birth defects after fathers were exposed to it (see Hydrocarbons on pages 131–2). Some of the toxic components of petrol can be absorbed through the skin — notably lead — so petrol should never be used for cleaning purposes, and splashes should be washed off immediately. Use unleaded fuel wherever possible and do not fill tanks in enclosed spaces. Avoid contact with petrol as far as possible if you are trying to conceive or are pregnant, since some of the hydrocarbons may cause birth defects and the lead may damage the developing baby's brain.

Pipes, copper
Copper is the standard material for gas and water pipes in the home. Under normal circumstances its use presents no hazard, but there is some suggestion that acidic water supplies may dissolve undesirable amounts of copper from the pipework. Hot water is more likely to dissolve copper than cold, so water for drinking and cooking should only be drawn from the cold tap (and should not come via a storage tank in the roof).

The method by which copper pipes are joined can cause a hazard. If soldered fittings are used, a reaction between the copper and the lead in the solder can result in potentially harmful amounts of lead dissolving in the water. For this reason pipes carrying drinking and cooking water should only be joined with compression fittings that do not involve lead. Straight soldered or capillary fittings should not be used on cold water pipes.

Pipes, lead
Many older homes contain lead pipes, especially the pipes leading from the water main to the household stopcock. Low levels of lead can be dissolved from these pipes and present a hazard to the health of young children, although in hard water areas this is less of a problem since lead does not dissolve very easily in hard water. The water supplier will test your drinking water for lead if you ask, and grants for replacement of lead pipework may be obtainable from your local council if EEC limits for lead in tap water are exceeded. These limits are rather high, however, so if you are having building work done anyway you should consider having the lead pipes removed, especially if your water

is soft. If you have lead pipes you should run the tap for a few minutes in the morning (and if you have been out all day) to flush out contaminated water before drinking or cooking with the water. Water filters do not generally remove dissolved lead.

Pipes, plastic
Plastic pipes are used widely for drains and waste water disposal from sinks, baths etc. They do not present a hazard in use, although in a fire some — especially **PVC** — can emit toxic fumes. If you are installing these pipes yourself you should be careful with the adhesive, which is inflammable and may emit toxic vapours. Plastic water supply pipes are becoming increasingly popular, but some types contaminate the water with traces of chemicals from the plastic. If you must use this type of pipe, ensure that it is approved by the water authority. In view of doubts about contamination from plastic pipes it is probably better to use copper where possible for water that people are likely to drink.

Putty
Putty consists of chalk and linseed oil, although in the past white lead has been added to speed up the drying process and some less reputable manufacturers may still do so. It may irritate sensitive skins but is generally non-hazardous. Rags used for wiping putty, which may become moistened with **linseed oil**, should be wetted after use and disposed of immediately to prevent spontaneous combustion. When removing old putty, assume it contains lead and clean it up thoroughly. Wash your hands and keep children away until the area is clean. Only buy traditional putty from well-known manufacturers. Some modern putties are based on **acrylics** rather than linseed oil and chalk. They may irritate the skin in use but are not especially hazardous.

Roofing felt
Roofing felt comes in many varieties, from a plastic film designed to sit under tiles or slates to a thick mineral-based material, used as an exterior surface on flat roofs. This latter type often consists of **bitumen** mixed with sand or small stones or fibres such as glass fibre or asbestos. The bitumen may present a cancer risk

if handled carelessly, so wear gloves when using it. Avoid the types that contain **asbestos**, as dangerous fibres can be released when the material is cut or abraded. Do not use water collected from a bituminised roof for drinking purposes or for watering vegetables. Plastic felt is inflammable but otherwise non-hazardous in these circumstances.

Rust treatments

Rust treatments fall into two main categories: those which remove or convert the rust and those which cover the metal surface with a waterproof barrier such as wax, bitumen or paint.

The former type may be a fairly strong acid. **Hydrofluoric acid** has been used in the past but this is extremely dangerous and has now largely been replaced with **phosphoric acid**. This can cause skin burns and is poisonous, so wear rubber gloves when using it, take great care not to get it in your eyes and wash any splashes off the skin immediately with plenty of water. Small burns and splashes on the clothing can be treated with sodium bicarbonate solution, but large burns need medical attention. Tannin may also be used as a rust treatment; this combines with the rust to form a stable surface, which can be painted. Tannin may be carcinogenic and is an irritant.

The latter type of rust treatment is not normally corrosive, but may irritate the skin. **Bitumen-based** products are more harmful as bitumen is carcinogenic. The solvents in which these products are dissolved are often inflammable and may be harmful by inhalation or when absorbed through the skin. Aerosol products may also contain inflammable propellants.

Sealant, acrylic

Acrylic sealants are water-washable compounds that harden on exposure to air to form a waterproof but slightly flexible seal. They may cause slight skin irritation in some individuals and should not be swallowed, but are generally of low hazard. In a fire they may emit toxic fumes.

Sealant, silicone

Silicone sealants resemble acrylic sealants but tend to be tougher and more resistant to water. Once cured they are inert but while they cure they emit acetic acid fumes, which are irritant. Do not get excessive quantities of silicone sealant on your skin and keep it out of your eyes — be careful when using pressurised dispensers.

Sealers, masonry
See Stabilisers.

Solder
Solder is an alloy of several metals that is designed to melt at low temperatures and combine with other metals to form a strong joint. Most solders contain **lead**, **tin** and some contain **antimony**. Lead is extremely poisonous and antimony is also toxic, so take care not to leave solder where children can get hold of it. Clear up any particles or drips after soldering and do not rub solder down with dry abrasives, as a toxic dust is produced. If you are pregnant or breast-feeding it is advisable to avoid using solder. If you have a hobby that involves soldering (e.g. jewellery-making or electronics) carry it out in a separate room and make sure that you do not take lead dust into the rest of the house on your hands or clothes. Solder should not be used on pipework carrying drinking water or in other circumstances where it can come into contact with food or drink. Some specialist solders with very low lead levels are available, and these are likely to be much safer.

Stabilisers
Stabilisers are used to seal and bind loose and flaky surfaces on stonework and other walls, often prior to painting. The simplest type is a water-based **polyvinyl acetate** (PVA) product that is sold as a general adhesive, sealant and stabiliser. This is used on interior walls for sealing flaking plaster, and some exterior products are based on a similar system. More powerful exterior products are solvent-based and leave a hard plastic resin in and on the treated surface. The hazards of the water-based type are principally skin irritation in sensitive individuals, although some products may contain a fungicide or mould inhibitor that is more toxic than the PVA. The solvent-based products, as well as irritating the skin, release fumes that are inflammable and harmful if inhaled. Wear gloves when using these products, and ensure

that there is plenty of ventilation when using the solvent type. Use eye protection if using either type on a large scale to prevent splashes or spray entering your eyes.

Stopper, flexible

This material is used to fill holes and cracks in external woodwork prior to painting. It is resin-based and contains a fungicide. It may irritate the skin and you should not inhale the dust when you rub it down. Stoppers for interior woodwork often contain solvents and may be inflammable as well as releasing possibly harmful fumes. Ventilation may be necessary while using them and you should avoid excessive skin contact if your skin is sensitive.

Tile restorer

This is an aerosol spray containing **sodium hydroxide**, designed to remove grease and dirt from ceramic tiles. It will irritate the skin, cause severe damage to the eyes and should not be used except where absolutely necessary and then only with protective gloves and goggles.

Tiles, asbestos cement

Some external roofing tiles are still made from **asbestos cement** and many existing tiles will be made from this material. They do not pose a significant risk to health if left untouched but during installation they may be cut and shaped with tools that produce large amounts of dust, which will inevitably contain asbestos. Do not use these tiles, and avoid cutting or abrading existing tiles of this sort. If you have to work with a large number of these tiles and are creating dust, wear a proper industrial dust mask — a simple DIY one will not do.

Tiles, polystyrene

These tiles, and similar products such as coving and ceiling roses, may present a fire risk as they are inflammable. They are particularly dangerous in a fire if painted with gloss or other oil-based paints. Avoid them, especially in kitchens above cookers, and never paint them with oil-based paints.

Underbody treatments

These products are used to protect the undersides of car bodies against rust. There are two main types: **wax** and **bitumen**. The wax type consists of waxes dispersed in a solvent, which coats the vulnerable parts with a water-repellent layer as the solvent evaporates. The other type achieves the same effect with bitumen. In both cases the evaporation of solvent poses fire and inhalation risks — **hydrocarbons** are the solvents normally used. The bitumen products pose an additional risk, since this material is carcinogenic. Use these products in well-ventilated conditions, wear gloves, eye protection and rough clothes, and wash off any splashes quickly with a hand cleaner. A barrier cream applied before starting the job can help. Do not breathe the spray or vapours.

Varnish

A varnish is a clear colourless or tinted coating applied to woodwork to protect and decorate it. Most modern varnishes are based on **polyurethane** and rely on chemical reactions between the ingredients as well as the drying of the solvent to form a tough film. The evaporating solvent — which is usually **hydrocarbon**-based — may be harmful if inhaled, so ensure you apply varnish in well-ventilated conditions. Interior versions are now available without added lead, but some exterior products may still contain lead and often contain fungicides. Older (pre-1987) interior products also contained lead, so do not rub them down dry or use blowlamps to remove old varnishes, as there may be a risk of absorbing excessive lead.

Some industrial two-part spray-applied polyurethane varnishes contain **isocyanates**. Do not use these unless you have been trained in their proper handling and have the correct lung protection, as they can be very dangerous.

Varnish remover

Some general-purpose paint strippers can be used to remove varnish, but there are specialist varnish removers on the market. These generally contain **dichloromethane, methanol** and **trichloroethylene**, all of which are poisonous. The mixture is inflammable and if the vapour is inhaled through a cigarette it will produce toxic breakdown products. Inhalation of the unburnt vapour is dangerous and can produce drowsiness. The mixture can also irritate the skin.

Wallpaper stripper
This contains a detergent that enables water to penetrate through the wallpaper and loosen the paste. It can irritate the skin, especially when undiluted, and you should avoid getting it in your eyes while applying it to the wall.

Water repellant
See Damp treatments.

Windscreen de-icer
These products are normally mixtures of **methanol** and **ethylene glycol** in an aerosol container. Both are toxic if swallowed, methanol especially so, and inflammable. Do not use these products in an enclosed garage as the vapours are toxic, and take great care not to get the spray in your eyes. Do not use while smoking. A safer alternative to aerosols containing methanol is the hand spray containing isopropanol — this is less toxic and the packaging is less harmful to the environment.

Windscreen wash
These products are added to the washer bottle to improve cleaning efficiency and prevent the contents from freezing in the winter. Some contain **ethylene glycol** and a detergent — the former is toxic and irritant — while others contain **ethanol** and **ammonia**, both of which are poisonous and irritate the eyes and skin. Keep the material off your skin, do not breathe the spray produced while the windscreen washer is operating and keep the material out of your eyes. The undiluted products are inflammable.

Wood bleach
See Wood lightener.

Wood hardener
Wood hardener is used to strengthen wood that has been attacked by wet rot and was subsequently dried out. It consists

of a volatile solvent such as **acetone**, which penetrates the pores
of the wood and impregnates it with a resin that hardens when
the solvent evaporates. It is highly inflammable and the vapour
is harmful, so ensure you use it only in well-ventilated areas.
The liquid may be irritating to the skin, but the dry product is
non-hazardous.

Wood lightener
The active ingredient of these products is a strong solution of
hydrogen peroxide. They are used to partially bleach wood,
and the peroxide solution is normally mixed with an activator
before application. The solution is corrosive and causes burns.
It will bleach and damage clothing. Wear gloves and eye protection when using these products and wash spillages off the skin
or clothes with plenty of water. Open the container with care
and be sure that you do not contaminate the peroxide solution
in the container with any other material as this may cause it to
decompose and produce a high pressure of oxygen beneath the
lid.

Wood stains
Wood stains for interior use consist of various coloured dyes
dissolved in a solvent, which evaporates as the stain dries. The
solvents are frequently **hydrocarbon** or **alcohol**-based and as
such are inflammable and may have harmful vapours. Some
exterior wood stains may be water-based and many contain
fungicides as well — these are often marketed as preservative
wood stains. Treat these with extra care, handling them as pesticides rather than decorative products.

Woodworm killer
Woodworm killers present two sources of hazard: the active
ingredient and the solvent. For many years **lindane** (gamma–HCH) and **dieldrin** have been used as active ingredients,
the latter mainly by professional pest control operators. Both are
toxic and persistent insecticides and lindane has been linked
with leukaemia (see under individual entries). More modern
formulations use **permethrin**, which is less persistent and, so far
as we know, likely to be less hazardous to humans and pets than

lindane or dieldrin. We recommend that you avoid lindane-based products.

Lindane and dieldrin are both highly toxic to bats and their use in roof spaces has been held responsible for a drastic decline in the bat population of Britain. As bats are protected species, to use lindane in a roof where bats are known to roost is illegal. The Nature Conservancy Council recommends permethrin and **cypermethrin** as alternatives.

All official approvals for the use of dieldrin were withdrawn on 30 March 1989. Any product containing this material still on sale is illegal.

The solvents in which these products are applied may also be harmful by inhalation, and may cause skin irritation. They are also often inflammable. If you have to use woodworm killers, do so with plenty of ventilation, wear protective clothing, eye protection and gloves, which are impermeable to the product in use. If you are working in an enclosed space — e.g. a cramped roof — wear proper respiratory protection and take frequent fresh air breaks. A simple dust mask will not protect you against these materials. Treated items of furniture should be allowed to dry out thoroughly before being used or placed in living accommodation and should not be used for the storage of food. Treated rooms should not be inhabited for at least a week unless the affected timbers can be sealed off, e.g. with a well-fitting hardboard floor or other impervious barrier. Cats should not be allowed to walk on uncovered treated floors and should not be left in recently treated rooms.

Some woodworm killers are used in conjunction with fungicides to treat dry rot — see Dry and wet rot treatments. There is no point in using a combined treatment if only one of the problems is present and there is every reason not to.

6.

A–Z LISTING OF CHEMICALS AND OTHER SUBSTANCES

Care is needed in interpreting toxicity data. It is important not to confuse 'toxic' with 'hazardous'. A chemical will be reported as 'highly toxic' if only a small amount is needed to produce the toxic symptoms. Whether or not a 'highly toxic' chemical is hazardous depends on how likely it is that that small amount will actually find its way into your body via the relevant route. Asphalt is an example of a substance that is toxic if swallowed, but since no adult is likely to attempt to eat a lump of tar the actual hazard this poses to him or her is really rather small.

The route of entry is of course an important factor, so too is the concentration of the chemical. You will see, for example, that we have listed benzalkonium chloride as an eye irritant, information that we have extracted from the standard texts on chemical toxicity. If you look at a bottle of a contact lens solution, you may find that this contains the very same chemical that we have listed as irritating to the eyes! The key to this apparent contradiction is simply the strength of the solution involved; in the contact lens fluid it is very dilute indeed, something like 0.004 per cent (or 40 parts per million, written 40 p.p.m.). The information in the toxicity textbook did not say how strong was the solution that irritated the eyes of the unfortunate rabbit it was tested on, but we can assume it was a good deal stronger.

A lot of the toxicity data we reproduce is gathered from experiments on animals, and this is often all there is to go on. We have already discussed some of the problems that come about when we try to apply data about cancer or birth deformities in animals to human beings. Are they a reliable indication or not? There are similar problems with interpreting data about acute toxicity too, though it is much more generally accepted that if a chemical proves to be highly acutely toxic to a mouse then it is right to treat it as highly acutely toxic to people. Some of the toxicity data are of course the result of 'experiments' on people; those who are routinely exposed to particular chemicals in the course of their work, or those who are accidentally exposed to a large amount in one go. Where the information is known to come directly from the experiences of people, then we say so.

HOW TO USE THE LIST

The list is arranged alphabetically by chemical name. After each name, you will find listed the main uses of the chemical which you are likely to encounter in the home or garden. If entries in this list are in **bold** type, then it means you will find further useful information about the particular chemical in the relevant section elsewhere in the book.

Next comes information about the acute toxicity of the chemical, and the most important routes by which it may enter the body.

Information about the longer term hazards comes next. If the chemical is known to be, or suspected of being, a carcinogen or teratogen, the entry will say so; likewise if the chemical is a mutagen.

Next we tell you what is known about the chemical's irritant or allergenic (sensitising) properties.

This is followed by any other information about the longer term health hazards of the substance, e.g. if it is an anticholinesterase compound, is suspected of suppressing the immune system, causes psychological problems, or is likely to damage a particular organ such as the liver or kidney.

Some chemicals pose little threat to human health or to the environment in normal circumstances, but may become dangerous in an accident, e.g. if mixed with other chemicals, or in a fire. These more unusual hazards are summarised next. We may also give information here about any synergistic effects (i.e. if one chemical's hazardous nature is magnified by the presence of others).

We next cover the environmental hazards that may be associated with the particular chemical.

The environmental data may be followed by precautions to be taken while using the chemical, e.g. to exclude people or pets from the area where the substance has been used for a specified time or to ventilate the area where it is used. Our inclusion of such information should not be taken to mean that we endorse the use of the particular chemical!

We may follow this with precautions to be observed when disposing of the substance after use.

Finally, we include any information known to us about restrictions or bans on uses of the chemical in other countries. Some chemicals are included which are either banned or restricted in this country too (or else are about to be), because you may still encounter them.

There is of course an enormous amount of data about chemical hazards, published in thousands of different books and journals, so no entry of ours can be truly complete. If, however, we have found that little seems to be known about the hazards of a particular chemical then we say so, lest you should assume from a very short entry that a chemical is 'safe'.

ALPHABETICAL LISTING

We have attempted to list all the common names of each chemical but the full hazard information is given only once. Other names of the chemical will refer you to the main entry. If you do not find the chemical you want it is possible that it is not listed under the first name you have; e.g. what we call acypetacs-zinc is occasionally called zinc-acypetacs. Numbers are ignored in deciding the position of a chemical in the index, e.g. 2,4,5-T comes at the beginning of the Ts.

Acetic acid In dilute form acetic acid is a comparatively mild acid, which provides the main flavour in vinegar. Acetic acid vapour is released as silicone sealants cure. The concentrated substance causes burns and is poisonous. More dilute solutions can irritate the skin and the vapour can irritate the eyes and breathing passages. People with sensitive skins may react more strongly to acetic acid. If affected, wash the area with sodium bicarbonate solution. Ensure ventilation as silicones cure.

Acetone A common household solvent used for removing grease, nail varnish and other stains. It is used as a solvent in some glues and wood hardener. Acetone is moderately toxic if swallowed or inhaled and can cause skin irritation. High doses produce drowsiness. It is inflammable and volatile. Use acetone in well-ventilated areas and keep away from sources of ignition.

Acypetacs copper, acypetacs zinc Wood preservatives and masonry biocides. Acypetacs zinc is one of the fungicides considered by the Nature Conservancy Council to be safe for use in roof spaces used by bats. The solvents used may however be toxic and treatment should not take place while the bats are in residence. We have no information on the toxicity of these compounds to people.

Alcohol See Ethanol, Isopropanol, Methanol.

Allethrin An insecticide for indoor or garden use. It is a mutagen. The chemical may cause contact dermatitis. It gives off irritant fumes when heated. Like all **pyrethroids**, it is toxic to fish and may be harmful to bees.

Alloxydim-sodium A weedkiller. Little is known of its toxicity and the World Health Organisation list it as an 'unknown hazard'. It is an irritant to the eyes and skin. A species of grass, *Poa annua* (meadow grass) has become resistant to this herbicide in some areas.

Alkylaryl ammonium chloride, alkylbenzyl ammonium chloride See Quaternary ammonium compounds.

Alphachloralose A **rat and mouse poison**. Listed by the World Health Organisation as 'moderately hazardous', it is toxic if swallowed and has a narcotic effect. It affects a wide range of wildlife: in small mammals it causes death by lowering of the body temperature. It also has a narcotic effect on birds and has been used as a bird repellent. Birds or animals (including pets) that feed on affected rats and mice may be poisoned by this chemical, and barn owls are known to have been killed by it. It has also been used in illegal poison bait for birds of prey. Professional operators using alphachloralose are recommended to wear a dust mask and **PVC** or rubber gloves. It must be kept out of reach of children and pets and should not be used outdoors.

Alphacypermethrin A household insecticide for professional use only. We have no information on its toxicity, but it is a **pyrethroid** and will therefore be a danger to fish.

Alum See Aluminium sulphate.

Aluminium A metal used for many purposes where lightness and strength are required, e.g. in **cooking utensils**. Aluminium compounds are added to some water supplies during treatment to remove suspended particles. Aluminium is not acutely toxic to humans, but it is dangerous to fish. Long-term exposure to aluminium at low levels has been linked with Alzheimer's disease, a brain disorder associated with old age. An incident in which a Cornish water supply was accidentally contaminated with aluminium sulphate caused a variety of health problems in consumers. These included memory loss, nervousness and irritation, and burns which probably resulted from the acid nature of the aluminium sulphate.

   Levels of aluminium dissolved in the water of lakes and streams have been found to have increased in some areas over the past few years: this is one of the most serious long-term effects of acid rain, which leaches the aluminium out of the soil once a certain critical point has been reached. The ecological effects of increased aluminium include the loss of fish and of birds such as the dipper which feed on water-borne insects.

Aluminium ammonium sulphate This compound is sold for garden use as a **slug killer** and mouse repellent. It is slightly acidic when damp and hence irritant if inhaled or swallowed. The damp powder could also be irritating to the skin, so you should wear gloves when handling it and avoid breathing any of the fine powder. You should especially avoid getting any of it in your eyes.

Aluminium chlorohydrate An active ingredient in many **deodorants**. It may be irritant, especially to cracked or damaged skin, and some people may have an allergy to it. It is very irritating to the eyes.

Aluminium sulphate (alum) A garden **slug killer**, sold in the form of a dry powder. When dissolved it forms a weak solution of **sulphuric acid**, and is therefore moderately toxic if swallowed or inhaled. It may also be a skin irritant if damp. Wear gloves when handling it, avoid breathing the powder and take care not to get it in your eyes.

Amines A group of chemicals with a wide range of uses, including fungicides and setting agents for resins. They vary in toxicity from slight to high and many are skin irritants. Some also cause sensitisation and allergy. Keep products containing amines off your skin and avoid breathing their vapours.

Aminotriazole A 'total weedkiller' that remains in the soil and is transported ('translocated') within plants. It is slightly toxic if swallowed, and the World Health Organisation consider it 'unlikely to present a hazard'. Its chronic effects are however a matter of some controversy. It is a probable human carcinogen and has a powerful action against the thyroid gland in animals. Animal experiments have also shown it to be fetotoxic and a teratogen. Aminotriazole has caused skin sensitivity in users. The chemical is banned in Norway and Finland and restricted in Sweden. In Britain it is very widely used by local authorities for the control of weeds on pavements and roadsides, although some councils have now decided to ban its use.

Ammonia A gas used in solution as a cleaning agent and disinfectant, sometimes with soap added ('cloudy ammonia'). The solution is poisonous and causes burns. The gas is a powerful irritant to the eyes and breathing passages and at room temperatures the solution gives off sufficient gas to cause a hazard in confined spaces. If heated or mixed with alkalis such as sodium hydroxide or many other household cleaners, much more gas is released. Wear gloves when using undiluted ammonia solution, do not breathe the vapour and keep it out of your eyes. Do not mix the solution with other cleaning agents. Wash splashes from the skin with plenty of water and see a doctor if the pain persists.

Ammonium hydrogen fluoride A wood preservative for professional use only. This chemical is highly toxic and irritant by swallowing, inhalation or skin contact.

Ammonium nitrate An artificial fertiliser. Ammonium nitrate is slightly toxic if swallowed, although it is much more dangerous to very young children because of its nitrate content. It is an oxidising agent which means it promotes fire, so it should not be mixed with any combustible material. When heated it may explode, so store it in cool places. Toxic fumes are emitted when ammonium nitrate is heated.

Ammonium oxalate Used in some chrome polishes. Ammonium oxalate is highly toxic if swallowed and, in its concentrated form, is a powerful irritant. Oxalates have a corrosive effect when swallowed and once absorbed cause damage to the kidneys. Minimise skin contact when using products containing ammonium oxalate and do not allow children to play with them. Do not get the material in your eyes.

Ammonium persulphate This chemical generates **hydrogen peroxide**, a bleaching agent, and is used in some cleaning products. It is moderately toxic if swallowed. Ammonium persulphate is a powerful oxidising agent and may thus react strongly with some other chemicals or combustible materials to create a fire hazard. It gives off toxic fumes if heated.

Ammonium sulphamate A **weedkiller** that is moderately toxic if swallowed. The World Health Organisation consider it 'unlikely to present a hazard'. It is an irritant to the skin or to the breathing passages or stomach if swallowed or inhaled. If burnt, the chemical gives off poisonous gases.

Ammonium sulphate This is used in mixtures with **ferrous sulphate** as a mosskiller. The chemical is moderately toxic if swallowed. It is a powerful oxidiser, so it must not be mixed with any inflammable material and should be stored carefully.

Ammonium thioglycollate An ingredient of some perm solutions. It is of moderate to high toxicity if inhaled or swallowed. It is a strong allergen and may cause contact dermatitis. It gives off highly toxic fumes on heating or on contact with acids.

Amyl acetate A solvent used in lacquers, nail varnish and some solvent mixtures. Amyl acetate is moderately toxic if swallowed or inhaled. High concentrations breathed for a long period cause irritation to the eyes, nose and throat, headache, fatigue and drowsiness. It is highly flammable. Use products containing amyl acetate in well-ventilated conditions away from sources of ignition.

Antimony A metal used in some solders. Antimony compounds are used in matches. Antimony and its compounds are highly toxic if swallowed or inhaled and can cause skin irritation. Avoid breathing the fumes from soldering and from burning matches.

Aromatic compounds Chemists use this term to describe certain chemicals related to and including the solvent **benzene**: others in the group include **toluene** and **xylene**. They are present in petrol and are used, individually or in mixtures, as solvents in a wide variety of products. As a group, aromatic compounds are often toxic by swallowing, inhalation or absorption through the skin. Some are carcinogenic and all are inflammable. Avoid exposure to these compounds where possible — see under individual entries.

Arsenic trioxide This chemical is found in some yacht anti-fouling paints. All arsenic compounds are highly toxic and are recognised human carcinogens. Many forms of ill-health may result from chronic exposure. On heating, the chemical forms toxic fumes of arsenic.

Asbestos A fibrous mineral used for insulation and in sheets or combined with cement as a construction material. It is also used in car brake and clutch linings and has been used as the backing to plastic tiles. There are three basic types of asbestos, blue, brown and white. All forms of asbestos are extremely dangerous if inhaled, although blue asbestos is regarded as being the most harmful. Large amounts of asbestos clog up the lungs and cause a disease called asbestosis. A much smaller exposure causes lung cancer and a cancer of the chest wall called mesothelioma. Smokers are especially vulnerable. The use of asbestos in many products has been curtailed in recent years, but there are still thousands of tonnes of asbestos in buildings throughout Britain. Identifying and removing it is a specialist task and you should consult your local environmental health department for advice if you think you have asbestos that needs removing. Intact asbestos can be painted over but it should never be sanded, drilled or sawn. Crumbling asbestos may need removal. Old cookers may contain asbestos in their walls or door seals — seek specialist help if particles or lumps are loose.

Asphalt A solid form of **bitumen**, less inflammable and hazardous than the more liquid forms.

Atrazine Atrazine is a total **weedkiller** that persists in the soil and is taken up by plants through the roots. The World Health Organisation list it as being 'unlikely to present an acute hazard in normal use'. It is moderately toxic if swallowed and may have a cumulative effect. It is a mutagen and embryotoxic to rats at high doses. Atrazine is a slight skin and eye irritant and some people may have a strong allergic reaction to it. It gives off poisonous gases on heating. It is very widely used by local authorities and others. Some weeds are becoming resistant to the chemical. It may have adverse effects on soil life; populations of springtails have been shown to be reduced by its use. It is also harmful to aquatic life in low concentrations. Atrazine is a persistent pesticide and has become a widespread contaminant of water supplies. The chemical has been included in the government's draft 'red list' of water pollutants needing special control measures.

Bacillus thuringiensis A bacterial insecticide, licensed for indoor use by professionals only, and an amateur garden product. Little is known of its toxicity, but there is no evidence of any harmful effects apart from very slight skin and inhalation irritancy to mammals.

BCF (bromochlorofluoromethane) See Halons.

Beeswax A general purpose wax used in polishes. It may cause allergy in some people and will burn if heated sufficiently.

Benazolin A weedkiller and growth regulator which the World Health Organisation consider is 'unlikely to present an acute hazard in normal use'. It may be a mild skin and eye irritant. It gives off toxic fumes on heating. Benazolin is harmful to fish.

Bendiocarb A **carbamate** insecticide. A **household pest control** product sold in various aerosol sprays for killing ants, wasps and cockroaches. The World Health Organisation rate this as a 'moderately hazardous' pesticide; it is highly toxic if swallowed and may be absorbed through the skin. It is an anti-cholinesterase agent. Bendiocarb may produce highly toxic fumes of **MIC** (methyl isocyanate) if heated in a fire. It is dangerous to fish, game and wild birds, and toxic to honey bees. This product should never be used in a confined space and all contact with the skin, eyes and mouth must be avoided. If you do get any on the skin or in your eyes then wash it off immediately and wash hands and other exposed areas of skin after use in any case. It may be hazardous to children or pets 'if incorrectly used'.

Benomyl A garden fungicide. The World Health Organisation rate it as 'unlikely to present an acute hazard in normal use'. It is only slightly toxic if swallowed. It is a mutagen and a possible carcinogen and teratogen in laboratory animals. The chemical has caused skin rashes and is a moderate sensitiser and allergen. If used repeatedly benomyl may build up in the soil and has been shown to be harmful to earthworms and other soil animals. Many fungal pests have become resistant to it. It is slightly toxic to fish and the US Environmental Protection Agency list it as a wildlife hazard. It is banned in Finland and from garden use in Sweden.

Benzalkonium chloride A quaternary ammonium compound used in disinfectants and other cleaning products and also in wood preservatives. It is highly toxic if swallowed, and is a skin and eye irritant. If any of this chemical should be swallowed then rinse out the mouth at once and drink plenty of water or milk, then get the help of a doctor.

Benzene An aromatic solvent found in many petroleum mixtures e.g. petrol. Benzene is acutely toxic, causing excitation then depression and breathing failure. It is more significant as a chronic poison, since repeated exposure to small quantities causes a wide range of symptoms including fatigue, headache, dizziness and weakness followed by pallor and bleeding from the nose and gums. It attacks the blood system, causing anaemia and, in some cases, leukaemia. Benzene is a skin irritant and is absorbed through the skin, although it normally causes problems when inhaled. It is highly inflammable. Pure benzene is not used in DIY or other household products, but may be present in mixtures. Avoid exposure to all petroleum vapours as much as possible and ensure that any such products are used with plenty of ventilation.

Benzene hexachloride See HCH.

Benzoyl peroxide A curing agent for polyester resins, e.g. in two-part wood fillers, usually used as a paste containing 50 per cent water. Benzoyl peroxide is moderately poisonous if swallowed and is an irritant. It is a powerful oxidising agent and may cause a fire if mixed with combustible material, particularly if it has been allowed to dry out. Keep benzoyl peroxide off your skin and away from flammable material. Clean up any spillages promptly.

BHC See HCH.

Bioallethrin An insecticide for household and garden use. It is highly toxic if swallowed. We have no other information on its toxicity. Being a **pyrethroid** it should be presumed toxic to fish.

Bioresmethrin A **pyrethroid** insecticide for garden use and licensed for household pest control by professionals only. The World Health Organisation list it as 'unlikely to present an acute hazard in normal use'. It is highly toxic if inhaled and moderately so if swallowed or absorbed through the skin. At high doses it is fetotoxic in rabbits. It is very toxic to bees and harmful to fish.

Bitumen A tarry liquid or semi-liquid material used as a sealant, waterproofer, adhesive, carpet tile backing, roofing material and pesticide. Bitumen is toxic if swallowed, but this is unlikely to happen in normal use. It may irritate the skin and is a low-level carcinogen. Bitumen is also inflammable. Wear gloves when using bitumen and keep it off your skin. Despite recommendations to do so, do not line water tanks with bitumen in case toxic materials leach out of the lining.

Bleaching powder See Calcium hypochlorite, sodium hypochlorite.

Borax See Boric acids.

Boric acids Insecticides and fungicides for garden use and the treatment of timber and masonry. The acid itself is not used, but various of its derivatives are. The sodium salt, sodium tetraborate or disodium octaborate ('borax'), is widely used in timber preservatives and also as an insecticide against **ants**. It is moderately toxic if swallowed and a dose of five to ten grams can be sufficient to cause the death of a child. The other boric acid derivatives that are commonly used are the organoboron esters, which are effective as both fungicides and woodworm killers. These compounds have low toxicity but may be irritant to the eyes. There is some evidence that exposure to boric acid compounds may lead to reduced fertility. Borax and some of the organoboron esters are among the pesticides considered by the Nature Conservancy Council to be safe for use in roof spaces inhabited by bats. Bear in mind however that the solvents used may have toxic properties, and treatment should not take place while the bats are in residence.

Brodifacoum A **rat and mouse poison**. Brodifacoum is the most potent of the newer anticoagulant poisons and is not licensed for use by householders.

Bromadiolone A **rat and mouse poison**. A powerful anticoagulant, which is moderately toxic if swallowed. Cases of poisoning in children have apparently occurred. It is a potential hazard to pets and wildlife, especially birds of prey.

Bromophos A general soil insecticide, also licensed for household pest control by professionals only. The World Health Organisation rate bromophos as 'slightly hazardous'. It is a mild anti-cholinesterase agent that can be absorbed through the skin. It is moderately persistent and harmful to wildlife, including bees. It is also dangerous to fish. At least one product on sale to the public states on the container that you do not need to wait to harvest vegetables after using bromophos, but this conflicts with the Ministry of Agriculture's published advice that there should be an interval of at least seven days before harvesting.

Bupirimate A garden fungicide. It is moderately toxic if swallowed. The World Health Organisation list it as 'unlikely to present an acute hazard in normal use'. It can be irritating to the eyes and skin. It is harmful to fish.

Butane A hydrocarbon gas used as a heating fuel, for portable blowlamps and as a cigarette lighter fuel. It is a component of LPG motor fuel. Butane is not particularly toxic if inhaled in small quantities, but may cause drowsiness. Large doses have proved to be fatal to solvent abusers and it can cause suffocation in confined spaces by excluding oxygen. It is highly inflammable. Avoid breathing excessive amounts of butane and keep it away from naked flames, cigarette ends and sources of electric sparks.

Butanol A solvent used in various mixtures. Butanol is moderately toxic if inhaled, swallowed or absorbed through the skin. It may cause eye irritation, headache and dizziness and dermatitis. It is inflammable. Keep butanol off your skin and use it in well-ventilated conditions.

Butanone See Methyl ethyl ketone.

Butoxycarboxim An insecticide marketed as 'Plant Pin'. It is moderately to highly toxic if swallowed and it can irritate the eyes, but there is little other information on its toxicity.

Butyl alcohol See Butanol.

Cadmium A heavy metal. Cadmium and its compounds are used in metal plating, rechargeable batteries and as pigments in industrial paints and pottery glazes. These substances are highly toxic, both acutely and chronically. The effects of moderate amounts of swallowed cadmium resemble food poisoning, while repeated low doses accumulate and cause damage to the heart, kidneys and liver. Inhaled cadmium damages the lungs severely. There is some evidence that very low levels of cadmium intake have reproductive effects, reducing the growth rate of the foetus and leading to a lower weight at birth. Poisoning from cadmium in the home is unlikely, although some foodstuffs may be contaminated. Possible domestic sources include orange or red enamelled cookware, especially if it is old, car paints, and rechargeable batteries. Avoid these sources and if you are uncertain about your cookware, ask your environmental health department for advice. Some cheap imported toys may contain cadmium in the paint: see Chapter 3.

Calciferol An ingredient in some rat and mouse poisons that has a synergistic effect with **warfarin**. On its own calciferol (vitamin D_2) appears to have a low toxicity to people but is highly toxic to dogs. If using warfarin baits you should in any case take great care to ensure that pets cannot reach it. We do not know if the inclusion of calciferol in the bait will increase the risk of secondary poisoning (i.e. if a cat, dog or wild bird or animal feeds on the intended victim) but it seems likely that this will be the case.

Calcium carbonate Natural chalk, used in putty and as a food additive, sometimes for nutritional purposes. Virtually harmless.

Calcium hypochlorite (bleaching powder) An ingredient of cleaning products. Calcium hypochlorite is highly toxic if swallowed or inhaled and is a powerful irritant. It emits highly toxic **chlorine** gas. It may explode if mixed with acids and is an oxidising agent, so should be kept away from inflammable materials. Wear gloves when using products containing bleaching powder and keep if off your skin. Take care not to inhale the dust. Wash any material off the skin or out of the eyes with plenty of water and seek medical help if the pain persists.

Calcium plumbate A **lead** compound used in priming paints, mainly for metal window frames etc. Calcium plumbate is highly toxic if swallowed or inhaled and the lead may be absorbed through the skin. It is a suspected carcinogen. Do not use this material and prohibit contractors you may employ from doing so. Use wetted sandpaper for rubbing down metal windows, and clean up the debris scrupulously.

Calomel (mercurous chloride, mercury (I) chloride) A fungicide restricted by EEC legislation to the control of **club root**, white rot of onions, and as a **lawn treatment** for dollar spot and *Fusarium*. While less toxic than other mercury compounds, calomel is poisonous if swallowed and is rated by the World Health Organisation as 'moderately hazardous'. The chemical is a mutagen. It is harmful to fish. The release of all mercury compounds into the environment should be avoided since they may be changed into more hazardous forms and may accumulate in living organisms.

Captan A fungicide used in seed dressings and **rooting powders**. It is slightly toxic if swallowed and the World Health Organisation rate it as 'unlikely to present an acute hazard in normal use'. Captan is a mutagen, carcinogenic in animals, a suspect teratogen and has proved toxic to the embryo and foetus in animal experiments. Other chronic effects are known, including effects on the liver and kidneys of test animals. It is a skin and lung sensitiser, irritant to the eyes and to the stomach and can cause skin rashes. It is harmful to fish and other water life in very low concentrations. This pesticide has been withdrawn in Finland, Norway and Sweden. If using products containing captan you should be careful to avoid accidentally contaminating your skin or eyes or breathing any in. If you do get any in your eyes you should wash them in cold water for fifteen minutes and see a doctor if irritation persists.

Carbamates A class of insecticides (with some other uses): many are moderately to highly toxic if swallowed and some may also be absorbed through the skin. Some are carcinogenic, teratogenic or mutagenic. Many carbamates affect blood cholinesterase levels.

Carbaryl A carbamate insecticide with several garden uses, including **lawn treatments**. It is also used in **shampoos** for head lice and fleas on pets. It is very toxic if swallowed and moderately so when absorbed through the skin. The World Health Organisation list carbaryl as 'moderately hazardous'. It is a mutagen and is carcinogenic and teratogenic in laboratory animals. Other chronic and reproductive effects have been found, and it is an anticholinesterase compound. It is a skin and eye irritant. Carbaryl is moderately persistent in the environment and the Soil Association consider it to be one of the pesticides most responsible for bee deaths. For this reason the Ministry of Agriculture advise that it should never be applied to a crop that is in flower. It is also poisonous to earthworms and harmful to fish and other water life in very low concentrations. It is reported to be more toxic to dogs than to other animals. Published harvest intervals vary between one week for apples and pears and six weeks for strawberries. In view of the poisonous nature of this chemical its use is best avoided; if it is used you should certainly take great care to avoid getting any in your mouth or on your skin and use appropriate clothing and gloves (see Chapter 2). Carbaryl has now been banned in West Germany.

Carbendazim A garden fungicide, wood preservative and masonry biocide. The chemical is moderately hazardous if it comes into contact with the skin. The World Health Organisation consider that it is 'unlikely to present an acute hazard in normal use'. It is mutagenic and a carcinogen in animals; it is also embryotoxic at high doses in animal tests. It is moderately persistent in the soil and harmful to fish. If using timber treatments containing carbendazim, you should wear protective gloves and eye protection and ensure thorough ventilation. Pets and children must be kept out of the treated area while the chemical is drying. When used on crops in the garden, the recommended harvest interval is up to fourteen days depending on the crop.

Carbolic acid See Phenols.

Carbon dioxide A gas that is naturally present in the atmosphere in small amounts and is not toxic. It may in certain circumstances be an asphyxiant, causing unconsciousness or death through lack of oxygen. The only domestic uses of carbon dioxide are in fire extinguishers and sparkling drink makers. Globally, the rising level of carbon dioxide in the atmosphere (more than 25% increase in the last 100 years) is the most significant cause of the 'greenhouse effect'. This is causing the earth to become warmer at a much faster rate than has ever been the case before. There is a danger that this will result in major disruption to the climate, increasingly frequent weather catastrophes and a rise in sea levels around the world. The rise in carbon dioxide levels has happened because humanity has been burning coal, gas and forests on a massive scale. Energy conservation is one of the best preventive measures.

Carbon monoxide Carbon monoxide is a gas that is formed when fuels such as coal, gas, petrol or wood are burnt inefficiently. It has a dangerously toxic effect on the human body by preventing the blood from carrying oxygen to the brain. This is a particularly hazardous form of poisoning because the first symptoms are drowsiness and perhaps a slight headache, which may then lead rapidly to unconsciousness and death. Several hundred deaths occur every year from carbon monoxide poisoning as a result of badly adjusted stoves, gas fires and solid fuel burners. It is most important to keep these well maintained with airways and flues clean and free from any obstructions. Carbon monoxide has adverse affects on health at much lower levels than those that can cause death. Headaches, dizziness and fatigue can all result from exposure to low levels of this gas. People who suffer from coronary artery disease, anaemia or stroke are more likely to suffer ill health from it than the general population. There is also some evidence from studies on rats that the growth of the developing foetus is slowed down by exposure of its mother to carbon monoxide — one of the arguments for not smoking during pregnancy. While carbon monoxide is mainly an indoor pollution problem, it is also one of the gases present in the exhausts of cars. The concentration of carbon monoxide in heavily trafficked streets, particularly those that are confined by tall buildings, may exceed the health guidelines laid down by the World Health Organisation, sometimes by a factor of several times.

Carbon tetrachloride A chlorinated solvent formerly used for removing grease and in fire extinguishers. Carbon tetrachloride is very poisonous if swallowed or inhaled and moderately toxic if absorbed through the skin. It is an irritant and a suspected carcinogen. Current DIY and household products do not contain carbon tetrachloride, but old ones may. Do not use them but contact your environmental health department for advice on their safe disposal.

Caustic soda See Sodium hydroxide.

CFCs See Chlorofluorocarbons.

Chlordane A persistent organochlorine pesticide. Chlordane was available to the general public until the end of 1988 for use as an earthworm killer on lawns. Chlordane is very toxic if swallowed and may be absorbed through the skin. The World Health Organisation classify it as a 'moderately hazardous' compound. It is a mutagen and a suspect human carcinogen and teratogen. Other serious chronic effects have been noted in both laboratory animals and human users of this chemical. It is an eye and skin irritant. It persists in soil, water and the body tissues of mammals. It is highly toxic to fish and other water organisms and dangerous to bees, livestock and birds. It is now illegal to sell chlordane for amateur use in Britain.

Chlorinated hydrocarbons A general term for organic chemicals containing carbon linked directly with chlorine. The group includes solvents such as **trichlorethylene** and **dichloromethane** as well as insecticides such as **chlordane** and **HCH**. Most of these substances are toxic to a greater or lesser extent: some extremely so. They are fat-soluble and may be persistent in the environment. Chlorinated hydrocarbon solvents may convert to the toxic gas **phosgene** when partially burned, e.g. if inhaled through a cigarette.

Chlorine A gas used for the disinfection of water. Chlorine is highly poisonous when inhaled and was one of the main gases used in the First World War. Small amounts cause irritation to the eyes, throat and lungs while larger amounts fill the lungs with fluid thereby causing death. Chlorine may be produced accidentally when **bleach** or bleaching-powder based products are mixed with acids such as toilet cleaners or some sink cleaners. For this reason, cleaning products should never be mixed.

Chlorofluorocarbons (CFCs) A class of compounds used for a variety of purposes including aerosol propellants, the working fluid in **refrigerators**, blown foam **packaging**, insulation materials and solvents for cleaning electronic components. CFCs generally have very low toxicity and this is one reason for their widespread use in the home and industry. A great deal of scientific detective work in the last few years has established beyond doubt that they are a threat to the earth's **ozone** layer. Some damage has already been done and may take centuries to repair; if it is not to get much worse before it gets better then the release of CFCs to the atmosphere must cease as soon as is practically possible. CFCs also contribute to the greenhouse effect (see Carbon dioxide), which is another reason for curbing their use.

Chloroxuron A herbicide sold for use in gardens as a **moss-killer**. It is moderately toxic if swallowed and the World Health Organisation list it as 'unlikely to present an acute hazard in normal use'. It is a potential skin and eye irritant. Chloroxuron is slightly toxic to birds. Because it is a general herbicide, care should be taken not to get it on nearby plants, which may be damaged. Avoid contact with the skin, do not breathe in any mist and do not get the chemical in your eyes.

Chlorpyrifos An **organophosphorus** insecticide that is moderately persistent and is sold for use as a general soil insecticide in gardens. It is very toxic if swallowed and may be absorbed through the skin. The World Health Organisation rate it as 'moderately hazardous'. This chemical is an anticholinesterase agent and a skin and eye irritant. It is dangerous to bees and fish and can be dangerous to birds and mammals.

Chlorpyrifos methyl An insecticide, licensed for household pest control by professionals only. The chemical is highly toxic if swallowed, and a skin irritant. It is dangerous to birds.

Citric acid A mild acid used in some cleaning products to remove hard water stains from stainless steel sinks etc. Citric acid is an irritant and may cause allergies in some people. Keep it off your skin and wash your hands after using it. Do not get it in your eyes. Splashes in the eyes should be washed out with plenty of water and medical help obtained if the pain persists.

Coal An unprocessed solid fuel. Coal dust is harmful if inhaled in quantity and the smoke produced when it burns contains a wide range of harmful materials, some of which are carcinogenic. It is illegal to burn ordinary coal in smoke-control areas, and this should be avoided anywhere in order to avoid pollution.

Coke A solid fuel obtained by processing coal. Coke burns much more cleanly than coal and most types are approved for use in smoke control areas. Petroleum coke should not be used in domestic fires, as it produces too much heat and may cause serious damage to the fireplace.

Copper naphthenate A fungicide that is a common ingredient of green wood preservatives. It is highly toxic if swallowed or inhaled and a moderate fire risk. Copper naphthenate is one of the chemicals that the Nature Conservancy Council consider safe to use in a roof where bats may breed or roost. The solvents used may however still be toxic to bats so the treatment should not be carried out while the bats are likely to be using the roof.

Copper sulphate A fungicide used with calcium hydroxide as 'Bordeaux Mixture' for the treatment of blight etc. It is moderately toxic if swallowed and the World Health Organisation list the chemical as 'moderately hazardous'. Chronic exposure may cause problems to the skin, eyes or lungs: eczema, conjunctivitis and pneumoconiosis have all been recorded in agricultural workers using it. Copper sulphate is mutagenic and a possible animal carcinogen. It is persistent in the soil and may cause damage to soil life if used repeatedly. Some mixtures are dangerous to bees. Copper sulphate is harmful to fish, livestock and animals.

Coumatetralyl A rat and mouse poison. This is one of the older anticoagulant chemicals, which kill rodents over a period of time after they have had several doses of the bait. Rats in some areas have acquired a resistance to anticoagulants. Where they have not yet done so this type of chemical should be used in preference to the much more powerful modern poisons such as **bromadiolone** and **difenacoum**, which pose a real threat to animals or birds that prey on the dying rodents.

Creosote A traditional wood preserver used on fences and other outdoor structures. Creosote is very poisonous by swallowing, inhalation or skin contact since it contains large amounts of **phenols**. Creosote is carcinogenic. Soil under fences repeatedly treated with creosote may contain phenol residues. Animals and plants can be harmed by contact with creosote, especially while it is still wet. Modern products are generally less harmful but if you must use creosote wear gloves, boots and protective clothing. Use eye protection if brushing it at a high level and keep children and pets away from treated areas until the wood is completely dry. Do not contaminate fish ponds.

Cresol A mixture of chemicals known as cresols is used to clean grease and dirt off car engines. Cresol solutions are also sold as fungicidal washes for use in gardens and greenhouses. Cresol is toxic if swallowed, inhaled or absorbed through the skin. It causes serious skin burns and smaller doses may cause allergic reactions in some people. Wear gloves, boots, eye protection and protective clothing when using products containing cresol.

Cresylic acid See Cresols.

Crocidolite (blue asbestos) See Asbestos.

Cuprous oxide A **yacht anti-fouling** agent. This chemical may be irritating to the eyes and breathing passages. All copper compounds are moderately toxic if swallowed.

Cyanoacrylates A group of chemicals used in fast-acting

adhesives. Cyanoacrylates are toxic if swallowed or inhaled and can be powerful irritants. They may produce allergic reactions in some people. Keep adhesives containing cyanoacrylates off your skin and avoid breathing the vapour.

Cypermethrin A wood preservative and insecticide for indoor and garden use. It has a high toxicity if swallowed. The World Health Organisation rate this chemical as 'unlikely to present an acute hazard in normal use'. There is evidence that it is carcinogenic in animal tests. It is a mild irritant and a possible skin sensitiser. Irritation of the lungs and damage to the eyes are two possible hazards arising from the use of cypermethrin. It is one of the chemicals considered safe for use in roof spaces where bats breed or roost. You should not however carry out any treatment while the bats are in residence as the solvent fumes may be harmful to them. If in doubt consult the Nature Conservancy Council (address in Chapter 7). Cypermethrin is extremely dangerous to fish and dangerous to bees.

2,4-D A selective herbicide sold in many mixtures, especially **lawn treatments**. If swallowed, 2,4-D is moderately to highly toxic, depending on the exact chemical formulation. The World Health Organisation list it as a 'moderately hazardous' compound. There have been many cases of acute poisonings among agricultural workers using this chemical and it has caused a variety of illnesses including skin and mucous membrane irritation and nervous disorders. It is a mutagen and a carcinogen and teratogen in animal tests. A study of farmworkers in the USA linked 2,4-D use with a rare form of cancer. It is highly irritating to the eyes. The chemical is harmful to fish. It is banned in Colombia, Guatemala, India and the USA. Several local authorities in Britain have discontinued its use.

Dalapon A weedkiller sold for use against couch and other grasses. Dalapon is moderately toxic if swallowed; the World Health Organisation list it as 'unlikely to be an acute hazard in normal use'. It is a corrosive chemical and there is a risk of skin and eye irritation. Wear gloves and protective clothing if using dalapon. If any of the chemical gets into the eyes, flush with cold water for several minutes and see a doctor if irritation persists.

DEET See Diethyl toluamide.

Deltamethrin A **pyrethroid** insecticide licensed for household pest control by professionals only. The World Health Organisation rate this chemical as 'unlikely to present an acute hazard in normal use'. It is irritating to the eyes and skin. Deltamethrin is extremely dangerous to fish.

Demeton-s-methyl A systemic **organophosphorus** insecticide that is available for garden use, despite being listed by the World Health Organisation as a 'highly hazardous' chemical. It is highly toxic if swallowed and is also absorbed through the skin. Demeton-s-methyl is a mutagen. It has caused birth defects and is embryotoxic in laboratory animals. It is an anticholinesterase agent. Demeton-s-methyl is harmful to bees, fish, livestock, game, wild birds and animals. Animals and poultry should be kept off treated areas for at least two weeks after use and no edible crops should be harvested for at least three weeks. It is banned from agricultural use in Russia.

Derris See Rotenone.

Diazinon A persistent **organophosphorus** insecticide sold as a garden product for use on soil pests, and as an insecticidal lacquer for use indoors. It is also used in some cat **flea collars**. Diazinon is a highly toxic chemical that can be fatal if swallowed and is readily absorbed through the skin. The World Health Organisation list it as 'moderately hazardous'. It is a mutagen and teratogenic and embryotoxic in laboratory animals. It is an anti-cholinesterase agent and a skin and eye irritant. The chemical gives off toxic gases on heating. It is dangerous to bees, harmful to aquatic life in extremely low concentrations and harmful to fish, livestock, game, wild birds and animals. Flies in some areas have become resistant to this chemical. Livestock and poultry should be kept out of treated areas for at least two weeks and no edible crops should be harvested for two weeks. Do not use the lacquer on surfaces where food is prepared or stored.

1,2-dibromoethane An additive to leaded petrol that helps to remove lead particles from the engine. It has also been used as a pesticide. 1,2-dibromoethane is highly toxic by any route of absorption and is carcinogenic. This material is one of the ingredients that make petrol toxic and make it dangerous to breathe petrol vapour or get excessive amounts on your skin. It is a subsidiary, although significant, reason for using unleaded petrol.

Dicamba A herbicide sold in many different mixtures for use as a **lawn treatment** and as a brushwood killer. It is moderately toxic if swallowed. The World Health Organisation list this chemical as 'unlikely to present an acute hazard in normal use'. There is evidence that it is a weak mutagen. It is a skin irritant and an eye irritant especially in mixtures with **mecoprop** (five products combine these two chemicals). Dicamba may be harmful to fish.

1,4 dichlorobenzene See Paradichlorobenzene.

Dichlofluanid A fungicide used in timber treatment and a yacht anti-fouling agent. It is moderately toxic if swallowed, a slight skin irritant and a moderate eye irritant. The World Health Organisation consider that it is 'unlikely to present an acute hazard in normal use'. There is evidence that it is a mutagen. The chemical is harmful to fish. It should not be used where children may come into contact with the chemical.

Dichloromethane (methylene chloride) A chlorinated hydrocarbon solvent used in paint removers. Dichloromethane is moderately toxic and its main exposure route is by inhalation. High concentrations in the air cause sleepiness, dizziness and tiredness, particularly if exposure is prolonged. It may have serious adverse effects on people with heart disease. Dichloromethane is a powerful skin irritant, producing a burning sensation within seconds of contact. It is carcinogenic in animals and may be weakly teratogenic. There are few data on its effects on human reproduction. Keep dichloromethane off your skin and out of your eyes — prolonged washing with water is necessary if contact occurs and you may need medical attention. Only use products containing this material in well-ventilated conditions and do not have any naked flames present, as large amounts of highly toxic phosgene may be produced as the vapour partially burns.

Dichlorophen This chemical is used as a moss and algae killer in several garden products, including lawn treatments, and for the control of fungi and moulds on walls and other surfaces indoors. It is moderately toxic if swallowed and is listed by the World Health Organisation as 'slightly hazardous'. The chemical has caused skin and eye irritation, cramps, diarrhoea and may be a skin sensitiser or cause dermatitis in some people. Dichlorophen should be kept away from pets (though in the correct dose it is a veterinary medicine used for deworming). If using it as a masonry treatment wear proper protective clothing and keep the area well ventilated.

Dichlorprop A herbicide sold in several mixtures as a **lawn treatment** or general weedkiller. It is moderately toxic if swallowed or absorbed through the skin, and the World Health Organisation list it as 'slightly hazardous'. It is an irritant of the skin, eyes and breathing passages. These dangers may be increased by the addition of **mecoprop**; some garden products combine these two chemicals. Dichlorprop is harmful to livestock (and therefore presumably to pets) and may also be harmful to fish.

Dichlorvos An **organophosphorus** insecticide of low persistence. It is used on impregnated resin blocks as a **fly-killer**, as a general insect killer in homes and greenhouses, and is combined with other chemicals in insecticide sprays. It has also been used in **flea collars** and sprays for cats and dogs. This is a very toxic compound that is poisonous if swallowed, absorbed through the skin or inhaled. The World Health Organisation list dichlorvos as 'highly hazardous'. It is a mutagen and a possible carcinogen. Dichlorvos is a potent anticholinesterase agent, though the effects are only short-term in most people. It is toxic to fish and bees. Houseflies and other pests are becoming resistant in some areas. In the USA, products containing dichlorvos are required to be labelled to warn against using them in rooms where infants, sick people or the old are confined, and in areas where food is prepared. In Britain users on farms or in glasshouses are advised to keep out of treated areas for twelve hours. Most slow-release fly-killers for indoor use are now fitted with shutters, which should be kept closed when they are not actually needed.

Dieldrin An organochlorine insecticide widely used as a wood preservative for many years. It is rated by the World Health Organisation as 'extremely hazardous' and can poison by swallowing, inhalation and skin absorption. In animals it is carcinogenic, embryotoxic and causes birth defects. There have been many cases of ill health brought about by the use of dieldrin in timber treatments in buildings. Dieldrin is very persistent and concentrates in food chains. It is a serious environmental pollutant responsible for declines in many bird of prey species, otters, etc. Although banned from all agricultural use for over ten years it is still present in many rivers and can render eels unfit for human consumption. In Britain a total ban on this chemical has been in force since March 1989.

Diethylene glycol A solvent used in some stain removers and possibly in some disinfectant products. This chemical is highly toxic if inhaled and is an animal carcinogen. It may have an irritant effect on the skin and should be kept away from the skin and eyes. In 1985 packaging manufacturers agreed to stop using it in the manufacture of cellulose wrapping for foods when it was found that the food could become contaminated.

Diethyl toluamide (DEET) The commonest active ingredient in insect repellants. This chemical is potentially highly toxic and should be used with care. It is very poisonous if swallowed and has caused death on several occasions. The more serious risk is that it may be absorbed through the skin in sufficient quantities to be toxic, especially in young children. Repeated application of quite weak solutions of DEET has led to brain disorders, nervous system effects and even death. There have been reports of severe skin irritancy or allergic reactions in adults caused by the repeated use of strong solutions. The stronger DEET solutions should not be used for young children, and 75 per cent solutions are adequate for even the most trying conditions in adults. These repellants should not be used extensively for days on end. The rate of absorption through the skin is increased by high temperatures and it is unwise to take a hot bath or sauna immediately after applying repellants.

Difenacoum A powerful anticoagulant **rat and mouse poison**. We have no information on the toxicity of this chemical to humans. Its use poses a potentially very serious threat to pets and wildlife, particularly barn owls, which in winter time may feed largely on rats and mice around farmsteads and buildings. Fewer than five poisoned rodents are sufficient to cause the death of an owl.

Dikegulac A weedkiller. Little information is available about this chemical. It apparently has a very low toxicity.

Dimethoate An **organophosphorus** insecticide with a systemic action. It is sold in a variety of garden chemicals, especially sprays against **aphids**. It is licensed for household pest control by professionals only. The chemical is very toxic if swallowed, inhaled or absorbed through the skin. It is listed by the World Health Organisation as 'moderately hazardous'. It is a mutagen and carcinogenic and teratogenic in animal tests. This chemical is an anticholinesterase agent. Dimethoate is harmful to a wide variety of wildlife: it is highly toxic to bees, harmful to fish and mammals, and birds feeding in a sprayed area may be killed. If dimethoate has been used, there should be a gap of one week before allowing access for livestock or poultry. No edible crops should be harvested for at least a week after use. Fully protective clothes should be worn by anyone using this chemical.

Dinocap A fungicide sold for use on roses. It is very toxic if swallowed. The World Health Organisation rate it as 'slightly hazardous' and it is a possible animal carcinogen. Dinocap may irritate the skin, eyes and breathing passages. Its use has caused allergic contact dermatitis. It is an acaricide (poisonous to mites) and toxic to fish. It is a moderately persistent chemical and if any edible crops are contaminated with it they should not be harvested for at least a week.

Dioxins A group of chemicals formed during the manufacture of certain compounds and the combustion of many others. The group contains some highly toxic materials, the most dangerous being the compound TCDD, sometimes simply known as 'dioxin'. The toxicities of some of this group are, at present, unknown. TCDD is toxic to some animals at extremely low levels and has also been found to cause cancers and birth defects in experimental animals. In humans, small exposures cause a severe skin rash known as chloracne. There is some circumstantial evidence of cancers and birth defects resulting from dioxin exposure. TCDD is widely regarded as one of the most noxious compounds discharged into the environment. Dioxins have no industrial or practical use but occur as contaminants in some herbicides (notably **2,4,5-T**) and are formed when chlorinated organic materials (e.g. **PVC** and chlorinated hydrocarbon solvents) are burned at moderate temperatures. High-temperature incineration will destroy dioxins but they are otherwise very difficult to break down and are persistent in the environment. To reduce the amounts of dioxins entering the environment do not burn PVC on fires or bonfires and, if your local authority incinerates domestic waste, avoid using disposable PVC products where possible (see Packaging in Chapter 3). Do not use 2,4,5-T weedkillers.

Diquat A general weedkiller. This chemical is related to **paraquat**, though it is considerably less hazardous. It may be fatal if swallowed, inhaled or absorbed through the skin; there is no known antidote. It has a variety of chronic effects on test animals, including reduced fertility and teratogenicity. Effects on people include eye and skin irritation (sometimes severe), damage to fingernails and delayed healing of wounds. Diquat is a very persistent chemical, being adsorbed onto clay particles in the soil but not broken down. Water should not be contaminated. It is harmful to animals and farmers are advised to keep livestock out of treated areas for at least a day. There is some disagreement as to how long after its use it may be safe to grow or pick crops: in Britain an official publication advises waiting four days before harvest, but one American guide suggests an interval of five months!

Disodium octaborate See Boric acids.

Diuron A herbicide used in total weedkiller granules. It is moderately toxic if swallowed and may irritate human eyes, skin and breathing passages. The World Health Organisation list this chemical as 'unlikely to be a hazard in normal use'. There is evidence of reproductive effects and teratogenicity in laboratory animals. It is also a possible animal carcinogen and one study in Sweden found an excess of cancers in workers using this chemical in mixtures with **aminotriazole**. Diuron is harmful to fish and should be kept away from children and pets.

Dodecylamine A fungicide and mould inhibitor. Dodecylamine is mildly toxic and alkaline. It may irritate the skin and eyes, so avoid splashes on these tissues. Do not mix it with **ammonia** solution as it will release large amounts of ammonia gas.

Dodecylbenzyltrimethyl ammonium chloride See Quaternary ammonium compounds.

EDTA (Ethylene diamine tetra-acetic acid) This is a complexing or chelating agent that fastens strongly onto metals and other chemicals and thereby makes them soluble and easier to remove. It is used as an ingredient in cleaning and disinfectant solutions and perhaps in some detergents. It is not particularly toxic, although laboratory tests have shown it to be a mutagen and a teratogen in some animals. Some concern has been expressed that EDTA and similar chemicals should not become significant contaminants of water because toxic metals might be picked up and become more mobile in the environment.

Epoxy resins Two-part resins used as adhesives and fillers. The cured resins are virtually harmless providing that they are mixed properly and there are no unreacted ingredients present. The uncured material is a powerful irritant and the vapour is toxic. The curing agents may be very toxic and also irritant.

Some people are allergic to uncured epoxy resins. If using large amounts of these materials do so in well-ventilated conditions. Keep both parts of the mixture off your skin and avoid contact with the mixed resin until it has thoroughly cured.

Ethanol (alcohol, ethyl alcohol) A volatile solvent used in various DIY and cosmetic products. The intoxicating component of alcoholic drinks. Ethanol is moderately toxic if swallowed or inhaled and may irritate the skin if undiluted. It is highly inflammable. Methylated and surgical spirits consist of ethanol and some water to which other ingredients have been added in order to make them undrinkable. When using products containing ethanol take precautions against fire and avoid breathing excessive amounts of the vapour.

2-ethoxyethanol (cellosolve solvent) A solvent used in cellulose paints. 2-ethoxyethanol is moderately toxic if swallowed or absorbed through the skin and is slightly toxic if inhaled. High concentrations of the vapour in the air may irritate the eyes. If using this material keep it off your skin, ensure reasonable ventilation and take precautions against fire.

Ethyl acetate A solvent used in lacquers, nail varnish and similar products. Ethyl acetate is moderately toxic if inhaled, swallowed or absorbed through the skin. It has an irritant vapour and is inflammable. Repeated exposure can cause damage to the eyes. Use ethyl acetate in well-ventilated conditions and avoid excessive skin contact. Take precautions against fire.

Ethyl alcohol See Ethanol.

Ethylene dibromide See Dibromoethane.

Ethylene glycol A solvent and the main constituent of antifreeze. Ethylene glycol is toxic if swallowed and may irritate the skin. It tastes sweet, so it is particularly important that children do not get hold of products containing this material and that it is kept secure from pets. Do not breathe the vapour if using a spray and keep it off your skin.

Ethyl glycol acetate (Cellosolve acetate) A solvent for cellulose paints. Ethyl glycol acetate is moderately toxic if swallowed, inhaled or absorbed through the skin and is a mild skin irritant. It is inflammable. Keep splashes off the skin, ensure thorough ventilation when using products containing this substance and take precautions against fire. If spraying it, wear eye protection.

Fenarimol A fungicide for use against mildew and blackspot. There is little information available on this chemical but it apparently has a low toxicity. It is a slight eye irritant in rabbits. Fenarimol is harmful to fish.

Fenchlorphos An **organophosphorus** insecticide licensed for household pest control by professionals only. It is moderately to highly toxic if swallowed, a teratogen in animal experiments and an anticholinesterase agent. When heated it may give off highly toxic fumes.

Fenitrothion An **organophosphorus** insecticide for household and garden use. It is very toxic if swallowed and moderately so if absorbed through the skin. The World Health Organisation list this as a 'moderately hazardous' chemical. It is an anticholinesterase agent and has synergistic properties, increasing the effect of other organophosphorus compounds (e.g. **dichlorvos**). Fenitrothion is a moderately persistent pesticide that is dangerous to bees and harmful to fish, livestock, wild birds and animals. If using the chemical, special care needs to be taken to keep it off the skin, as it is rapidly absorbed. Livestock should be kept out of treated areas for a week and no edible crops should be harvested for at least two weeks. In Russia, the use of this chemical is prohibited for persons under eighteen years old, pregnant women, lactating mothers, men over fifty-five and women over fifty.

Fenoprop A selective hormone weedkiller used in lawn treatments. It is moderately toxic if swallowed and a potential irritant of the eyes, skin and breathing passages. The chemical is a teratogen in laboratory animals. It may form toxic fumes on heating. We have no information on its effects on wildlife.

Ferric sulphate A mosskiller, apparently of very low toxicity.

Ferrous sulphate A mosskiller. It is moderately toxic if swallowed. There is evidence that it is a mutagen. The chemical is harmful to water life in very low concentrations.

Formaldehyde A soil steriliser and ingredient of resins, it is a gas which is normally used as a solution in water. The gas is highly toxic if inhaled; the solution is very poisonous if swallowed and is a powerful skin irritant. Formaldehyde causes cancer in animals and is a suspected human carcinogen. Repeated exposure to formaldehyde can cause sensitivity and some individuals are strongly allergic to it. Low levels of the gas can cause irritation to the eyes and throat as well as headaches. Some types of cavity wall insulation release formaldehyde gas and the material also escapes from some chipboards and plywood. It has been used as an ingredient of shampoo and it is sold as a soil steriliser. Avoid these products if you think you may be sensitive to them. Ensure adequate ventilation if products likely to release the material are present in the home and seal chipboard and plywood with varnish or paint if necessary.

Formic acid A pungent-smelling acid used for descaling kettles. Formic acid is highly toxic if swallowed, moderately toxic if inhaled and a moderate skin irritant. Keep splashes off your skin or out of your eyes — wash them off with plenty of water and seek medical help if the pain persists. Use products containing formic acid in reasonably ventilated conditions.

Furmecyclox An ingredient of some timber treatment products. We have found very little information on this chemical. It is apparently of low toxicity but may be a skin irritant.

Gamma HCH or gamma BHC See HCH.

Glutaraldehyde A disinfectant. Glutaraldehyde is moderately toxic and a skin irritant. Handle the concentrated material with care and keep splashes, whether concentrated or diluted, off the skin and out of the eyes. Wash with plenty of water in case of accident.

Glycol See Ethylene glycol.

Glyphosate A translocated total **weedkiller**. It is slightly toxic
if swallowed. The World Health Organisation list glyphosate
as 'unlikely to present a hazard in normal use'. The main
hazard associated with its use appears to be that it is a powerful eye irritant and a skin irritant. Users have reported skin
rashes and nausea. Although the action of this chemical is
short-lived, it does not break down in the environment but is
strongly adsorbed onto the soil and therefore no longer available to plants. It is harmful to fish. Edible crops should not
be harvested for five to twelve days (depending on the crop)
after use of glyphosate. Livestock should be kept out of treated
areas for five days and poisonous plants such as ragwort should
be removed.

Graphite A form of carbon used as a lubricant and in pencil
'lead'. Largely harmless although excessive inhalation can
damage the lungs and some people may be allergic to it.

Gypsum A mineral used in interior plasters. Gypsum is not
particularly toxic but the dust may irritate. Wear a dust mask
if you feel uncomfortable when mixing plaster or sanding down
large areas. The related material phosphogypsum releases
rather more radioactivity than ordinary gypsum — it may be
wise to avoid this, especially if your home is built of granite
or other materials prone to release radioactivity.

Halons A class of chemicals similar to the **CFCs** which are used
in **fire extinguishers**. Their toxicity varies considerably, from
halon 1211 which is virtually inert, to halon 1011 which
'should be considered at least as toxic as **carbon tetrachloride**'. The major disadvantage of halons is that they do
not break down until they reach the ozone layer. Most of them
contain bromine, which is even worse at destroying ozone than
the chlorine in CFCs. The halons may be up to a hundred
times more potent in this respect than the CFCs and there is
thought to be synergy between the two classes of chemicals.
Thus although the quantity of halons manufactured is comparatively small there is every reason to control and sharply

reduce their release into the atmosphere. Halon 14 contains no bromine and will not attack ozone.

HCH (gamma-HCH, gamma-BHC, lindane). HCH is a mixture of several closely similar chemicals. All are insecticidal but only one, gamma HCH or 'lindane', is now permitted for use within the EEC. It is a **chlorinated hydrocarbon**, very widely used as a garden and household insecticide and as a **woodworm killer**. It is very toxic if swallowed and can be absorbed through the skin. The World Health Organisation describe it as 'moderately hazardous'. The chemical becomes more toxic in a warmer environment. Gamma HCH is a mutagen and carcinogenic in laboratory animals. Reproductive effects have also been found. Cases of leukaemia have been suspiciously high among some workers exposed to the chemical. Other chronic effects include liver and kidney damage and aplastic anaemia. It is a potential irritant of the skin, eyes and breathing passages and a variety of allergic reactions have been reported. Mild poisonings and allergies have occurred in people exposed to lindane in recently treated buildings. Gamma HCH is a persistent chemical and is widespread throughout the environment. It is dangerous to bees and fish and toxic to mammals, especially bats: the use of lindane in roof timbers is considered to be a major cause of the decline in bat populations in Britain. It is also notably toxic to cats, which cannot remove the chemical from their bodies in the way that other mammals can. When used outdoors, official advice is to keep livestock away from treated areas for two weeks and not to harvest any edible crop for two weeks after use. Potatoes and carrots should not be sown in treated ground for 18 months. There are bans or severe restrictions on the use of gamma HCH in Bulgaria, Colombia, Hungary, Finland, Japan, Portugal and Thailand.

Heptenophos A systemic **organophosphorus** insecticide of brief persistence. It is of high toxicity when swallowed and is an anticholinesterase compound. Little else is published regarding its toxicity.

Hexamine A fuel for some camping stoves and ingredient of some resins. Hexamine is moderately toxic, although it is used medicinally. Some people are allergic to it but the main risk from hexamine occurs when it is heated or burned. **Formaldehyde** gas is evolved, and this is toxic. Do not use camping stoves that burn hexamine in confined spaces.

Hydrocarbons A group of substances consisting of carbon and hydrogen in various combinations. Hydrocarbons are used in mixtures or alone as fuels, solvents and sealants — examples include methane, butane, petrol, toluene and bitumen. They are all inflammable, some extremely so, many are toxic and some are carcinogenic. Unburnt hydrocarbons are emitted by motor vehicle exhausts and contribute to air pollution in urban areas. The hazards of particular compounds are discussed under their individual headings, but some general studies on hydrocarbons as a group have been carried out. The exposure of pregnant women to hydrocarbons may lead to an increased risk of birth defects, although the evidence is not clear cut. There may also be a risk of a rare genetic defect, called Prader-–Willi syndrome, in children born to fathers exposed to large amounts of hydrocarbons although, again, the evidence is not conclusive. Some people are very sensitive to hydrocarbons and react badly to them. These people should be especially careful to avoid petrol, natural and liquid gas, and certain hydrocarbon aerosol propellants and solvents.

Hydrochloric acid A powerful acid, also known as spirits of salts, used as a cleaner and corrosion remover on metal. Hydrochloric acid, in its concentrated form, is very poisonous if swallowed. It causes severe burns to tissues and has an irritant and toxic vapour. It will corrode many metals and gives off inflammable hydrogen gas while doing so. If using products containing hydrochloric acid wear eye protection, rubber gloves and protective clothing. Do not breathe the vapour. Wash splashes off skin or clothes immediately with plenty of water and seek medical attention if the pain persists. Sodium bicarbonate solution can be used to treat minor burns and spillages can be neutralised with washing soda. Do not put hydrochloric acid in metal containers. Keep the product cool, as warmth can cause a build-up of gas pressure in sealed containers. This gas, hydrogen chloride, is produced when PVC plastics burn.

Hydrofluoric acid A powerful acid formerly used as a rust remover and sometimes used for etching glass. This material is extremely corrosive and will eat its way through glass. It causes severe skin burns and has a highly toxic and irritant vapour. Avoid using products containing hydrofluoric acid but if you must, ensure that you do not get splashes on your skin or eyes. Wash any splashes away with plenty of water and seek immediate medical attention whether or not the pain subsides.

Hydrogen An inflammable gas, a principal component of coal gas. Hydrogen may be formed when metals react with acids and is produced if aluminium priming paints are contaminated with water. Car batteries release hydrogen as they are charged. It is not toxic but a mixture of hydrogen and air is explosive. Do not smoke, and extinguish any nearby flames when opening tins of aluminium primer; likewise if you see bubbles rising from a mixture of metal and acid or if you are charging batteries.

Hydrogen chloride A toxic and irritant gas formed when plastics containing chlorine — e.g. **PVC** — burn. Dissolved in water it forms **hydrochloric acid**.

Hydrogen cyanide A highly toxic gas produced when **polyurethane**, acrylic and other plastics containing nitrogen burn. It is one of the main toxic ingredients in the smoke that kills most people who die in house fires.

Hydrogen peroxide A bleach, mild disinfectant and oxidising agent. Hydrogen peroxide is toxic if swallowed and may irritate the skin. Concentrated solutions, such as those that are used as wood bleaches, can cause burns. It readily decomposes, releasing oxygen gas, so any hydrogen peroxide product that becomes contaminated should be discarded, as sealing the container again may lead to a dangerous build up of pressure. Sunlight and heat promote the decomposition of hydrogen peroxide, which is why it is sold in dark-coloured bottles; it should always be kept in these and stored in cool cupboards rather than on open shelves. Keep hydrogen peroxide solutions out of your eyes and take great care when using the stronger mixtures.

Hydrogen sulphide A gas smelling of bad eggs. Hydrogen sulphide is released from 'stink bombs' and as well as smelling foul it is very poisonous. Fortunately, we can smell it at concentrations below which poisoning occurs. Do not allow children to use stink bombs in confined spaces, as harmful concentrations of gas may build up.

Imidazoline An ingredient of many **air fresheners** and fabric conditioners. It acts by partially blocking the sense of smell. Its toxicology is unknown and there may be psychological hazards associated with the use of air fresheners.

Iodofenphos A persistent **organophosphorus** insecticide for household use against fleas and other insect pests. It has low to moderate toxicity if swallowed or absorbed through the skin. It is slightly toxic to bees and very toxic to fish.

Ioxynil A contact herbicide formerly on sale to gardeners in lawn treatments. It is highly toxic if swallowed and is listed by the World Health Organisation as 'moderately hazardous'. It is a mutagen and in test animals has caused thyroid tumours and teratogenic effects. Following a review of its toxicity it was withdrawn from garden use in 1988 and should no longer be available.

4-indol-3-ylbutyric acid A herbicide used in some rooting powders. The chemical is highly toxic if swallowed. It may produce toxic fumes on heating.

Iron sulphate See Ferrous sulphate.

Isobutanol (isobutyl alcohol) A solvent. Isobutanol is moderately toxic by swallowing and inhalation. It is a moderate skin irritant and is inflammable. Avoid excessive skin contact and do not breathe large amounts of vapour.

Isocyanates A group of compounds used in the manufacture of some two-part resins, specialist paints and sealing compounds. Isocyanates are toxic by swallowing or inhalation and can irritate the skin. These compounds are powerful allergens and sensitisers — someone initially exposed to a moderate dose can be very seriously affected with asthma-like symptoms after a second very small dose. If affected, avoid all exposure to these materials. Even if you are not sensitive to isocyanates, keep products containing them off your skin and avoid breathing the vapour.

Isopropanol (isopropyl alcohol) A solvent sometimes used in windscreen de-icers. Isopropanol is moderately toxic if inhaled or swallowed and is a slight irritant, although it can be much more damaging to the eyes. It is highly inflammable. Avoid excessive skin contact and do not breathe the vapour. Keep the material out of your eyes.

Isopropyl alcohol See Isopropanol.

Lanolin A type of grease obtained from wool, used in cosmetics, toiletries and some medicinal ointments. Lanolin may cause allergies and contain pesticide residues.

Lead A heavy metal which, with its compounds, has a wide variety of uses. Lead and lead compounds are extremely toxic if swallowed or inhaled and significant amounts can pass through the skin. Acute lead poisoning involves convulsions, coma and death, while prolonged exposure to much smaller amounts produces headaches, constipation or diarrhoea, tremors and confusion among other symptoms. Young children are particularly at risk, since very low levels of lead can impair their intellectual development. The main domestic sources of lead are water from lead pipes, paint, dust containing lead from vehicles and odd items such as curtain weights. Safety precautions are discussed under the appropriate product etc. headings, but remember to take particular care to protect children, babies and pregnant women from exposure to lead.

Limonene A synthetic compound that is added to many cleaning products, air fresheners etc. to provide a 'lemon' odour. It is a possible animal carcinogen.

Lindane See HCH.

Linseed oil An oil used, on its own or with other materials, as a wood finish. An ingredient of putty. Linseed oil may irritate and cause allergies in some people. If spread thinly on rags or wood shavings it may spontaneously combust. Avoid excessive skin contact if you are sensitive to linseed oil and damp down any rags etc. before disposing of them. Wrap them up tightly or seal in old tins to prevent their exposure to the air.

Malathion An **organophosphorus** insecticide. It is licensed for household pest control by professionals only and is available to gardeners in a large number of sprays and dusts for use against **aphids** etc. It is very toxic if swallowed and may be absorbed through the skin, though it is only weakly toxic by this route. The World Health Organisation list this chemical as 'slightly hazardous'. There is evidence of mutagenicity and possible carcinogenicity in animal tests. Malathion is an anti-cholinesterase agent. It is irritant to the skin and eyes and an allergen. Some pests have become resistant to this chemical. It is highly toxic to bees and other beneficial insects, and harmful to fish. An interval of one day before harvesting any food crops is recommended.

Maleic hydrazide A growth regulator used on turf and to prevent suckers in trees and shrubs. The chemical is listed by the World Health Organisation as 'unlikely to present an acute hazard in normal use'. Chronic effects in animal tests include damage to the liver and kidneys, and possible carcinogenicity (the picture is confused by possible impurities in the batches tested). It is a slight irritant. Poisonous gases may be produced on heating. Maleic hydrazide is weakly toxic to fish.

Mancozeb Fungicide. It is slightly to moderately toxic if swallowed. The World Health Organisation rate this chemical as 'unlikely to present an acute hazard in normal use'. There is evidence from animal tests that it is a carcinogen and teratogen. It is irritating to the skin, eyes and breathing passages. Mancozeb is harmful to fish. It is a persistent chemical and edible crops should not be harvested for one week (fruit) or two weeks (lettuces) after use.

MCPA A herbicide sold in a variety of products, including several **lawn treatments**. It is moderately toxic if swallowed and may also be poisonous by inhalation or by absorption through the skin. The World Health Organisation list it as 'slightly hazardous'. It is weakly mutagenic and there are reports of birth defects in test animals. The chemical is an eye irritant and there have been cases of dermatitis and allergic reactions in workers manufacturing it. MCPA can be harmful to livestock, and therefore presumably to pets and wild animals as well. It is not toxic to bees but may reduce the numbers of springtails in soil. It is fairly persistent and there is a risk that composts made with treated grass clippings will retain the chemical's herbicidal activity.

MDI See Isocyanates.

Mecoprop A herbicide included in a number of **lawn treatment** products. It is moderately toxic if swallowed and may also be toxic if absorbed through the skin or inhaled. The World Health Organisation rate this chemical as 'slightly hazardous'. It is a mutagen and embryotoxic and teratogenic in some laboratory animals. Mecoprop can cause eye irritation and in some formulations may be a skin irritant as well. Mecoprop's irritant properties may be increased when it is mixed with **dicamba** or **dichlorprop**.

Melamine A plastic resin used as a protective and decorative coating on wood. Melamine is not toxic or otherwise harmful in the form in which it is normally encountered. Some liquid products that harden to form a melamine layer are irritant and harmful by inhalation, so use these with care. When strongly heated or burned, melamine emits highly toxic **hydrogen cyanide** fumes.

Mercurous chloride See Calomel.

Mercury A silvery metal, liquid at room temperature, used in barometers and thermometers. Mercury and its compounds are extremely toxic, although mercury metal can be swallowed without major ill effects, since it is not easily absorbed from the gut. It is much more dangerous when inhaled, and it is readily absorbed through the skin. The symptoms of acute mercury poisoning are stomach pains, headaches, tremor and collapse but low-level chronic mercury poisoning is more difficult to detect. Common symptoms are nervousness, depression, vague fears, insomnia and worsening co-ordination of the limbs. Mercury is a cumulative poison — repeated small doses can build up in the tissues. Some mercury compounds are teratogenic. Mercury becomes especially dangerous if it combines with hydrocarbons to form compounds such as methyl mercury. These compounds are readily taken up by living organisms such as fish or shellfish and can accumulate in poisonous quantities. This was the cause of the Minamata Bay tragedy in Japan, when hundreds of people were poisoned, many fatally. There were also many cases of children born with cerebral palsy or other forms of brain damage as a result of the methyl mercury ingested by their mothers.

Mercury metal is especially dangerous in warm, unventilated conditions, and all mercury compounds emit dangerous fumes when heated. If mercury is spilt from a broken thermometer do not handle it or allow children to play with it. Gather it up using gloves (not a vacuum cleaner, which helps to vaporise it) and dispose of it safely. In the case of a larger spill — e.g. a broken barometer — ventilate the room, exclude children and contact your environmental health department or fire brigade immediately. Avoid products containing mercury wherever possible, especially during pregnancy.

Metaldehyde The active ingredient in slug pellets. Metaldehyde is very toxic if swallowed, and a child has died from a dose of three grams. The World Health Organisation list it as 'slightly hazardous'. The use of unguarded pellets is very hazardous to pets. In whatever way it is used the chemical poses a considerable risk of secondary poisoning to mammals and birds which may feed on the dead slugs and snails. Metaldehyde may pass still further up the food chain and deaths of owls have been recorded after use in cropped fields. The chemical is also dangerous to fish. An interval of at least a week is recommended before allowing poultry into treated areas. If a liquid form of the chemical is used on crops then they should not be picked for at least ten days.

Methane A hydrocarbon, the principal constituent of natural gas. Methane is not especially toxic but can cause death by asphyxiation if large amounts flood confined spaces. Its mixtures with air are highly explosive: a potent odour is added to natural gas to make it easier to detect gas leaks. Natural gas is a relatively pollution-free fuel compared with coal or oil. It burns more efficiently, has a lower sulphur content, and does not form dangerous trace pollutants such as **polycyclic aromatic hydrocarbons**. Methane is released into the environment by rotting vegetation — 'marsh gas' — and the action of gut bacteria in cattle and other ruminant animals. It is increasing in the atmosphere and is a secondary, though important, cause of the greenhouse effect (see Carbon dioxide). When organic material is buried in landfill sites, methane may be generated in considerable quantities and migrate underground some way from the actual tip site. This is causing major problems at some sites, and a house in Derbyshire was recently destroyed in an explosion caused by landfill gas.

Methanol (methyl alcohol) A solvent and ingredient of de-icing mixtures and paint strippers. Methanol is highly toxic if swallowed and many deaths and injuries have occurred when people have mistaken it for ethanol and added it to drinks. Exposure to methanol, either in one large dose or repeated smaller doses, damages the optic nerve, eventually leading to blindness. It is eliminated from the body only slowly, so daily small doses can build up and have a cumulative effect. Methanol is toxic by inhalation and skin absorption. It is highly flammable. If using products containing methanol wear gloves, ensure plenty of ventilation, keep the material out of your eyes and take precautions against fire.

Methiocarb A **carbamate** compound used in a slug killer. It is highly toxic if swallowed and moderately so if inhaled. The World Health Organisation list it as a 'moderately hazardous' chemical. It is an anticholinesterase agent. It is harmful to fish and breaks down to form toxic substances that can be dangerous to animals. Methiocarb must be kept away from children, pets and fish. Poultry should be kept out of treated areas for seven days and no edible crops should be picked for seven days.

Methoprene An insecticide used for the control of fleas on pet bedding etc. Its toxicity is apparently very low and we have found no published references to any chronic effects.

Methyl alcohol See Methanol.

Methylated spirit See Ethanol.

Methyl chloroform See 1,1,1-trichloroethane.

Methylene chloride See Dichloromethane.

Methylene dichloride See Dichloromethane.

Methyl ethyl ketone (butanone) A solvent. Methyl ethyl ketone is moderately toxic if inhaled and slightly toxic if swallowed. It is a mild skin irritant and is highly flammable. Ensure adequate ventilation when using this substance and avoid excessive skin contact. Take precautions against fire.

Methyl Isocyanate (MIC) See Isocyanates.

Molybdenum A metal, the compounds of which are used in lubricants. Molybdenum compounds may be mild irritants, but in the form in which they are likely to be encountered in the home — greases and some oils — they are unlikely to be hazardous. When using any grease, avoid excessive skin contact and use a barrier cream if appropriate.

Naphtha A solvent used, for example, in paint brush restorers. Moderately toxic if inhaled, naphtha is a narcotic substance and exposure to the fumes may result in symptoms resembling drunkenness. Naphtha is inflammable.

Naphthalene Used in mothballs. Moderately toxic if swallowed, naphthalene is also poisonous by inhalation and absorption through the skin. It is a possible animal carcinogen and toxic to aquatic life in very low concentrations.

1-naphthylacetic acid Plant growth regulator. This chemical is moderately toxic if swallowed and a moderate irritant to the skin, eyes and mucous membranes. Chronic exposure can cause depression.

2-naphthyloxyacetic acid Presumed moderately toxic if swallowed. No other information on toxicity.

Natural gas See Methane.

Nicotine An insecticide, cleared for garden use but now marketed in only one product, Synchemicals' 'XL All Insecticide'. The World Health Organisation consider nicotine to be a 'highly hazardous' substance. It is extremely toxic if swallowed: as little as forty milligrams can cause death. It is also rapidly absorbed through the skin. Nicotine has been found to cause cancer and birth defects in animals and is a mutagen. It is dangerous to mammals, birds, fish and other aquatic life, and to bees. It is however not persistent, which is the reason why it was at one time permitted for use by organic growers; it is now prohibited by the Soil Association. If using nicotine you should cover the skin and wear neoprene or similar gloves. Wash off any splashes immediately. Do not allow any people, pets or livestock access to the treated areas for at least twelve hours. Do not harvest any edible crop for at least two days. See Aphids, p. 58.

Nitrates Fertilisers and drinking water contaminants. The significance of nitrates in drinking water as a public health risk is a matter of great controversy. Nitrates themselves have a low degree of toxicity, but once taken into the body in food or water undergo chemical changes to form nitrites, which in turn may form very small quantities of **nitrosamines**. Nitrites can poison the blood and starve the body of oxygen, a condition known as methaemoglobinaemia. Infants are most at risk from this; it is sometimes called 'blue baby syndrome'. It is a most uncommon disease in Britain, but bottle-fed babies are sometimes considered to be at risk in high nitrate areas. Nitrosamines are also a potential health risk because they are known to be carcinogenic in many different species of animal and are linked by some researchers to stomach and oesophageal cancers in people. The evidence for this link is uncertain; nevertheless the World Health Organisation considers that 'exposure . . . should be kept as low as practically achievable', and has set a recommended limit of fifty milligrams of nitrate per litre of drinking water. This is also the EEC directive standard fixed in 1980. This is not always achieved in Britain, especially in East Anglia and part of the Midlands. Precautions to minimise the health risk from nitrates include breast-feeding babies, not smoking, plenty of fresh fruit and vegetables to keep up the intake of vitamin C, and a high standard of oral hygiene (as bacteria in the mouth transform nitrate to nitrite).

If you use nitrate fertilisers they should be stored with care as they are oxidising agents and may promote fires or form explosive mixtures with other chemicals. They should be stored in bags rather than airtight containers, in cool dry conditions.

Nitric oxide See Nitrogen oxides.

Nitrogen dioxide See Nitrogen oxides.

Nitrogen oxides At least three distinct chemical compounds are brought together under this heading: nitrous oxide (N_2O), nitric oxide (NO) and nitrogen dioxide (NO_2).

Nitrous oxide is a narcotic gas sometimes used as an anaesthetic ('laughing gas'). The only domestic use of nitrous oxide is as an aerosol propellant in some food products, e.g. whipped cream. The gas is moderately toxic if inhaled and has long-term health risks associated with it: it is an experimental teratogen and a mutagen. In people, it has been shown to have an effect on blood pressure. These hazards are unlikely to concern you unless you are an anaesthetist or a professional cake decorator! On a global scale nitrous oxide is generated in large quantities by the use of nitrate fertilisers and their eventual breakdown by bacteria in lakes, rivers and the sea. The release of nitrous oxide into the environment is a cause for concern because it does not break down and is a 'greenhouse gas', contributing to the process of global warming (see Carbon dioxide).

Nitric oxide and nitrogen dioxide are products of combustion. Nitric oxide is formed first and some of this is rapidly converted in the air to nitrogen dioxide, so both gases are usually present together. For this reason, in any discussion of pollution from the burning of fossil fuels, you will usually see mention of 'oxides of nitrogen', sometimes written as NO_x. In this case, NO_x means only nitric oxide and nitrogen dioxide, not laughing gas.

The main ways in which you are likely to be exposed to NO_x are through cigarette smoking, from **gas cookers** and bottled gas heaters, and from heavy traffic (see Petrol). NO and NO_2 are acutely toxic in concentrations of 100 parts per million or more, causing oedema of the lung, which may lead to death. This concentration is a hundred times greater than the maximum that is likely to be found in even the worst-ventilated kitchen, and would only ever be encountered in an industrial accident. Much lower concentrations may however pose a threat to health. Nitrogen dioxide in particular is an irritant gas. It can penetrate mucous membranes and affect breathing and has been linked with increased susceptibility to respiratory infections. There is some concern that NO_2 can aggravate asthma even if the exposure to elevated levels of the gas is a fairly short one. The World Health Organisation recommends that hourly levels should not exceed 400 micrograms per cubic metre. The long-term effect on the lungs of repeated exposures above this level are uncertain and damage may be irreversible. This level may be exceeded in poorly ventilated kitchens with gas cookers or in city centres in rush hour traffic.

Nitrogen dioxide and nitric oxide are released in huge quantities from power stations and motor vehicles. They cause serious environmental damage by contributing to acid rain (see Sulphur dioxide) and, along with **hydrocarbons**, generating **ozone** and other pollutants in the lower atmosphere.

Nitrocellulose An ingredient of cellulose paints. Toxicity data are unavailable but nitrocellulose probably has a stimulant effect on the heart, which might be dangerous to people with heart disease. It is highly inflammable and, when dry, may explode. Take great care to avoid fire when using nitrocellulose, avoid excessive skin contact and do not breathe the spray.

The solvents in which nitrocellulose is dissolved (e.g. **toluene** and **xylene**) may also be hazardous. Never allow nitrocellulose paints to dry out in the can.

Nitrosamines A group of chemicals which may be formed in the stomach following the intake of **nitrates** in the diet. Nitrosamines have been shown to cause cancer in a great many animal species and the International Agency for Research on Cancer has concluded that some are probably carcinogenic in humans.

Nitrous oxide See Nitrogen oxides.

NTA (Nitrilo triacetic acid) A chelating agent, considered at one time as a possible alternative to phosphates in detergents. Chelating agents are however capable of binding to heavy metals, raising fears that highly toxic metals such as **mercury** and **cadmium** could be scavenged from sewage sludge or river sediments and remobilised in the environment. NTA is also carcinogenic in laboratory animals. It has been voluntarily withdrawn from detergent products in the USA.

Organoboron esters See Boric acids.

Organochlorines See Chlorinated hydrocarbons.

Organophosphorus compounds Organic compounds into which phosphorus has been incorporated. They include some of the most toxic chemicals ever manufactured, the nerve agents, some of which have now been used in warfare in the Gulf war. Many organophosphorus compounds have insecticidal properties. Their high acute toxicity stems from their action against cholinesterase, a vital enzyme in the body that regulates the functioning of the nervous system.

Ortho-phenyl phenol See 2-phenyl phenol.

Oxalic acid A mild acid sometimes used to restore the colour of wood. Oxalic acid is highly toxic if swallowed or inhaled and is a powerful skin irritant. Keep this material off your skin and out of your eyes and take care not to breathe any dust or spray when using it. Wear gloves and wash thoroughly any contaminated clothing.

Oxidising agents (oxidisers) These are substances that assist fire by providing extra oxygen to burning materials. Examples include **nitrates**, **sodium chlorate** and strong solutions of **hydrogen peroxide**. Ensure that these substances do not mix with combustible materials such as wood shavings and dust, paper, rags, sulphur, oils etc., as they may ignite with very little provocation.

Oxytetracycline hydrochloride A yacht anti-fouling agent. This substance is an antibiotic (kills bacteria) and is also used as a medicinal drug. Its toxicity is low. The problems with antibiotics are that they interfere with the natural balances that serve to keep disease-causing organisms in check and bacteria may quickly become resistant to them. For these reasons the release of antibiotics into the environment seems undesirable.

Ozone Whether ozone is a good thing or a bad thing depends entirely on where it is. It is a pungent gas that is formed naturally in the lower atmosphere by lightning flashes and by the reactions of **nitrogen oxides** and **hydrocarbons** in sunlight. The amounts of these chemicals in the atmosphere have risen greatly over the last few decades as a result of industrial pollution and the enormous increase in the number of motor vehicles, so the level of ozone has risen too. One estimate is that the air we breathe in Northern Europe now contains twice as much ozone as it did last century. Trace quantities of ozone are irritant, attacking the mucous membranes and the eyes, and may cause persistent headaches. Ozone also attacks materials, particularly rubber, and may damage vegetation. Ozone (perhaps in combination with acid mists) is now thought likely to be the main cause of the dramatic sickness of the forests in southern West Germany. There is a World Health Organisation recommended limit of 100 parts per billion, which is likely to be exceeded several times a year on sunny days in the south of Britain.

About fifteen kilometres above sea level, the nature of the

atmosphere changes suddenly. This higher part of the atmosphere is called the stratosphere and it is much richer in ozone. For this reason it is also known simply as the 'ozone layer'. The ozone layer fulfils an essential role in protecting life on the surface of the earth from the intense ultraviolet rays of the sun. If it were not there then there would be a massive increase in skin cancers, blindness, damage to the immune system and damage to crops and marine life. We now know that the ozone layer is being damaged by the transport into the stratosphere of **chlorofluorocarbons**, **halons** and certain solvent vapours. This has resulted in a loss of probably three to four per cent of the ozone over the most densely populated parts of the northern hemisphere as well as the much-publicised Antarctic ozone hole.

Ozone may sometimes be an indoor air pollutant if you work with electrical machinery. Rooms where photocopiers are kept switched on all day, for example, are places where the concentration of ozone can build up to a point where it is damaging to your health.

Parachlorometacresol A masonry biocide and yacht anti-fouling agent that is highly toxic if swallowed; it is also an allergen. The chemical is dangerous if heated, as it gives off highly toxic fumes of **phosgene**. We have no information on its long-term environmental effects.

Paradichlorobenzene (1,4-dichlorobenzene) An insecticide for household pest control and an ingredient in toilet freshener blocks. Paradichlorobenzene is highly toxic if swallowed. It has been reported to cause cancers in laboratory animals and also to cause liver injury in people following chronic exposure to the chemical. It is also a mutagen. It is persistent in the water environment and is a candidate for eventual inclusion in the government's 'red list' of chemicals that must, because of their toxicity and persistence, have their inputs to the environment greatly reduced.

Paraffin A hydrocarbon fuel, also known as kerosene. Paraffin is moderately toxic if swallowed or inhaled and a mild skin irritant. Repeated exposure may cause dermatitis in some people. It will burn on a wick or if soaked on rags but is difficult to ignite unless heated. The use of paraffin stoves may lead to indoor air pollution and condensation if ventilation is inadequate. Avoid excessive skin contact with paraffin and do not breathe the vapour. Never use petrol in an appliance intended for paraffin as an explosion may result.

Paraquat A **weedkiller**. According to the World Health Organisation, paraquat is a 'moderately hazardous' chemical. It is extremely toxic if swallowed — it has killed even when spat out — and has no known antidote. It can also be absorbed through the skin. It has caused various reproductive problems in laboratory animals and is a mutagen. Exposure to small amounts can lead to skin rashes, inflammation of the eyes, delayed healing of wounds and damage to fingernails. The chemical has been linked with aplastic anaemia. Paraquat is persistent, binding to clay particles in the soil rather than breaking down. It is harmful to aquatic life and toxic to mammals; it has poisoned hares in sprayed stubble. Paraquat is banned in Finland and West Germany, and restricted in the Philippines, Sweden, Turkey and the USA.

PCBs See Polychlorinated biphenyls.

PCP See Pentachlorophenol.

Penfenate Insecticide for household pest control. No toxicity data found.

Pentachlorophenol (PCP) A **wood preservative** and masonry biocide. The World Health Organisation rate this chemical as 'highly hazardous'. PCP is highly toxic whether swallowed, inhaled, or absorbed through the skin. It is also irritating to the skin, eyes and mucous membranes. PCP has caused chloracne in users (see Dioxins). Chronic exposure leads to liver and kidney injury. PCP is a teratogen and possible carcinogen in laboratory animals and immune system effects have been reported as well. It has been responsible for dramatic reductions in the sperm count of healthy men exposed to the chemical by sleeping on PCP-treated mattresses. Its toxicity is complicated by the possible presence of **dioxins** in some products. Many adverse health effects have been reported by people whose houses or workplaces have been treated with it. PCP gives off dangerous fumes in a fire; these too may contain dioxins and the same applies to timbers that have been treated with it. The chemical is very harmful to aquatic life, and many fish kills have been recorded following contamination of water with PCP.

PCP should never be used in anything other than very well ventilated conditions. Often people are told that they may return to treated premises within twenty-four hours, although traces of the chemical may be present in the air for months afterwards. Many researchers feel that twenty-four hours is far too short a time, especially where babies or young children are concerned. In the USA, the Environmental Protection Agency have altogether banned the use of pentachlorophenol in inhabited buildings.

Pentachlorophenyl laurate Wood preservative and masonry biocide. No toxicity data found; presume the hazards are as for **pentachlorophenol**.

Pepper Mouse repellent. The substance is irritating, especially to the eyes. Safrole, a constituent of black pepper, is a mutagen and animal carcinogen.

Perchloroethylene (tetrachloroethylene) A solvent used as a dry-cleaning fluid and in various other cleaning products. It is moderately toxic if swallowed, inhaled or absorbed through the skin. The liquid can cause injury to the eyes. At high concentrations the vapour may have a narcotic effect and be irritating to the eyes and throat. Repeated or prolonged contact may cause dermatitis. The chemical has been shown to cause cancer in laboratory animals and to be a mutagen. It may accumulate in the body and there has been a case of a child becoming seriously ill because the mother regularly visited a dry cleaners' premises and passed on perchloroethylene in her breast milk. Perchloroethylene gives off toxic fumes on heating. It is toxic to aquatic life in very low concentrations. Like all solvents, perchloroethylene should only be used in very well-ventilated conditions. Thoroughly air dry-cleaned clothing before storing it in living or sleeping rooms and do not transport it in unventilated cars.

Permethrin A **wood preservative** and insecticide for household and garden use. The World Health Organisation consider that permethrin is 'unlikely to present a hazard in normal use'. It is moderately toxic if swallowed, and a mild skin and eye irritant. It is listed as a possible carcinogen by the US Food and Drug Administration (FDA). Permethrin is one of the woodworm treatments recommended by the Nature Conservancy Council for use in roof spaces where bats may breed or roost, as it has low toxicity to mammals. It is however dangerous to bees and extremely dangerous to fish.

PET See Polyethylene terephthalate.

Petrol See Chapter 5, page 88.

Petroleum distillates See Hydrocarbons.

Phenols Phenols are a group of **aromatic compounds** that are used as disinfectants and are found in wood preservatives such as **creosote**. All of them are, to a greater or lesser extent, corrosive and dangerous if splashed on the skin or into the eyes. Phenol (carbolic acid) itself is highly toxic if swallowed: one and a half grams has caused death. It is also poisonous by skin absorption, which occurs rapidly. Chronic exposure can lead to kidney and liver damage. Phenol gives off toxic fumes on heating, and can react dangerously with oxidising materials. It is hazardous to aquatic life.

Phenothrin Insecticide for garden use and household pest control. It is moderately toxic if inhaled and can emit acrid fumes on heating. Little data available. It is a pyrethroid, and must therefore be presumed highly toxic to fish.

2-phenylphenol (ortho-phenyl phenol; biphenyl-2-ol; 2-biphenylol) A wood preservative and masonry biocide. A powerful disinfectant and fungicide also used, for example, on the peel and wrappers of citrus fruit. This chemical is moderately toxic if swallowed, and an irritant. It has mutagenic properties. It gives off acrid smoke and irritant fumes on heating.

Phosgene A highly toxic gas that may be formed by burning or heating organic compounds containing chlorine (e.g. **PVC** or **trichloroethane**). Used as a poison gas in the First World War, concentrations as low as fifty parts per million may be fatal after short exposure, causing death by damage to the lungs. It is highly irritating to the eyes and irritating to the mucous membranes; however it has little irritant effect on the respiratory tract so there may be no warning that a toxic gas is being inhaled. There is thus some risk of poisoning occurring by, for example, drawing fumes of a chlorinated solvent through a lighted cigarette.

Phosphates Ingredients of most **detergents**. Their toxicity to humans is low, and concern centres on environmental effects. Once in rivers, lakes or the sea, phosphates cause eutrophication (enrichment of nutrient supplies) which may, in certain circumstances, lead to the formation of algal blooms and eventual loss of oxygen from the waters.

Phosphoric acid Phosphoric acid is used as a rust remover. It is a corrosive chemical, highly toxic if swallowed and irritant if inhaled. It is dangerous if spilt onto the skin or splashed into the eyes. Phosphoric acid gives off toxic and irritant fumes when heated. It is harmful to aquatic life.

   Wear rubber gloves when applying the chemical, and take particular care not to get it in your eyes. Small burns may be treated with sodium bicarbonate solution, but if a large area is affected you should see a doctor at once.

Phoxim An **organophosphorus** insecticide, sold as an ant-killer for house or garden use. Little toxicity data is available: phoxim should be presumed to be an anticholinesterase agent and at least moderately toxic if swallowed. It is of brief persistence and has no systemic action. Phoxim is toxic to bees that come into contact with it or breathe the fumes.

Piperonyl butoxide A synergist added to pyrethrins or pyrethrum to increase their effect. It is highly toxic if absorbed through the skin, less so if swallowed. It has been shown to cause cancer in animals, although in the US the Environmental Protection Agency has concluded that it is not carcinogenic to people.

Pirimicarb A **carbamate** insecticide, sold as a greenfly killer, including an aerosol formulation. Rated by the World Health Organisation as 'moderately hazardous', pirimicarb is very toxic if swallowed and an anticholinesterase agent. It gives off toxic fumes if heated. Pirimicarb is harmful to livestock but apparently safe for bees. The harvest interval, depending on the crop, is up to two weeks.

Pirimiphos An **organophosphorus** insecticide, licensed for household pest control by professionals only. No toxicity data found: assume the hazards are no less than for **pirimiphos-methyl**.

Pirimiphos-methyl An **organophosphorus** insecticide, rated by the World Health Organisation as 'slightly hazardous' — it is moderately toxic if swallowed and may be absorbed through the skin. There is evidence of mutagenicity. Some formulations are irritating to the eyes and skin. It is an anticholinesterase compound. The chemical is dangerous in a fire as very toxic fumes are given off when it is heated. Pirimiphos-methyl is moderately persistent and dangerous to fish and bees.

Plasticisers A group of chemicals added to polymers such as **PVC** to make them tougher and more flexible. Several different chemicals are used in this way. Dioctyl phthalate, the one most widely used in Britain, has been shown to be carcinogenic and teratogenic in test animals. These chemicals can migrate from **packaging** into food, and in Italy packaging containing plasticisers has been banned from use with fatty foods. Some plasticisers are persistent chemicals and there are reports of them becoming contaminants of the water environment in some parts of the world.

Polyalkylene glycol ethers A range of chemicals used as brake fluids. They have low toxicity if swallowed, but some may be irritating to the skin or eyes.

Polychlorinated biphenyls (PCBs) A class of industrial compounds having many uses, PCBs have been gradually withdrawn since 1970, when it was realised that they are persistent in the environment and may concentrate in food chains. The different members of the group ('alachlors') have somewhat different toxicities, but all are moderately to highly toxic by swallowing, inhalation or absorption through the skin and all are suspected human carcinogens. Chronic exposure is reported to have caused chloracne (see Dioxins) and damage to the liver. Their toxic effect on the liver is synergised by **carbon tetrachloride**. PCBs give off extremely toxic fumes containing **dioxins** when heated or burnt at temperatures below 1200°C. Although manufacture of PCBs has all but ceased in Europe and North America and they have only been used in closed systems (such as capacitors and transformers) for many years, these chemicals continue to cause problems in the environment. They have been implicated in the decline of seal populations in the North Sea and levels remain high in coastal dwelling birds of prey.

PCBs are unlikely to be encountered in the home except in old capacitors used as starters in fluorescent lights, so these should always be disposed of carefully.

Polycylic aromatic hydrocarbons (PAHs) A group of chemicals found in tars and formed when many complex organic chemicals are incompletely burned. This group contains substances such as benzo-a-pyrene, anthracene and chrysene, which are common ingredients of smoke. Many of these materials are carcinogenic, some of them powerfully so, and exposure to atmospheric ozone is thought to increase their potential for causing cancer. Motor vehicles, especially badly tuned ones, emit these materials.

Polyethylene (polythene) Plastic material widely used in packaging etc. This material and the fumes it gives off when burnt are of low toxicity. It is an environmental problem because it does not degrade except by the action of strong sunlight. Some polythene products now have chalk mixed in to promote their breakdown into small fragments when they are buried.

Polyethylene terephthalate (PET) A plastic material that has become very widely used in recent years in drinks containers. We have found no toxicity data on this material, but it is relatively inert and PET bottles contain no plasticisers. It is not particularly hazardous when burnt as the compound is chlorine-free; the most toxic combustion product is therefore likely to be **carbon monoxide**. The material is very slow to degrade and PET bottles are aesthetically objectionable rather than polluting. PET could in theory be recycled.

Polypropylene A polymer that can be spun into tough fibres and has many applications as baler twine, fishing nets and cables, etc. It is of low toxicity but emits highly toxic fumes when burnt. Polypropylene is highly persistent in the environment. This is not a problem of chemical toxicity, but it is a hazard because birds, fish, marine mammals, etc., may swallow or become entangled in the fibres.

Polystyrene A plastic with many applications. Although it has been shown to be carcinogenic in animals, there are no toxic hazards associated with the use of polystyrene unless it is in a fire. The vapours produced are irritating and highly toxic if inhaled. Some expanded polystyrene foams, used for insulating packaging, may contain **chlorofluorocarbons** (CFCs).

Polyurethane Used in varnishes. Polyurethanes are carcinogenic in animal tests. It is however unlikely that any significant amount will enter the body in normal use and the solvents in which they are dissolved are the greater hazard. Polyurethanes give off highly toxic fumes containing cyanides if burnt.

Polyurethane foam Foam for packaging and **furniture**. It is a positive animal carcinogen. The major concern about the hazards of polyurethane foam is its behaviour in a fire. It ignites easily and burns fiercely, emitting dense black smoke and extremely toxic fumes containing cyanides. Many deaths in household fires are directly attributable to the use of this material in furnishings.

Polyvinyl acetate (PVA) Adhesive. Used in water-based products of low toxicity.

Polyvinyl chloride (PVC) PVC is a versatile plastic, which can be made into a rigid or a soft material. It is widely used in food **packaging** and also as a building material. PVC itself is of low toxicity, but the chemical from which it is made, the **vinyl chloride** monomer, is a known human carcinogen that is highly irritating to the skin and eyes or if inhaled. The monomer, or the **plasticisers** that are also present in packaging materials, may contaminate food wrapped in PVC film.

PVC is highly hazardous if burnt, giving off fumes that may contain **phosgene, dioxins** and **hydrogen chloride**. Plastic packaging, mouldings, or offcuts of PVC should never go onto bonfires.

Potassium permanganate A moderately toxic chemical if swallowed, irritant in dilute solutions and corrosive in stronger ones or in crystalline form. This chemical is a strong oxidising agent and could therefore promote or cause fire in mixtures with other chemicals. Potassium permanganate is permitted for use in some circumstances as a fungicide in organic agriculture, but it was not cleared for use as a pesticide by either the Ministry of Agriculture or the Health and Safety Executive in 1988.

Potassium phenylphenate (or phenoxide) See 2-phenylphenol.

Propachlor A weedkiller, rated by the World Health Organisation as 'moderately hazardous'. It is highly toxic if swallowed and may be absorbed through the skin. If taken in, it accumulates in the body. Propachlor is a mutagen, listed by the Equal Opportunities Commission as a reproductive hazard for women. The chemical may produce skin sensitisation in susceptible people. It is a potential hazard in a fire as it produces very toxic fumes on heating.

Propane A **hydrocarbon** gas widely used as a portable fuel supply. It is not toxic, but may cause unconsciousness or death by asphyxiation in a confined space. It is very inflammable and may form explosive mixtures with air. Propane gas is stored in red cylinders, as opposed to butane cylinders, which are blue. Appliances designed for use with the one should never be used with the other. Keep propane away from naked flames, cigarette ends and sources of electric sparks.

Propiconazole A systemic fungicide, listed by the World Health Organisation as 'moderately hazardous'. It is irritating to the eyes and skin. Propiconazole is harmful to bees and dangerous to fish. There is a minimum harvest interval of four weeks when it is used on cereals.

Propoxur A **carbamate** insecticide for household pest control. The World Health Organisation list this chemical as 'moderately hazardous'; it is very toxic if swallowed and is an anticholinesterase agent. Tests on animals have shown embryotoxicity and effects on the liver. The chemical is also a mutagen. It is highly toxic to bees and harmful to livestock, birds, animals and fish. Edible outdoor crops should not be harvested for seven days if propoxur has been used.

PVA See Polyvinyl acetate.

PVC See Polyvinyl chloride.

Pyrazophos An **organophosphorus** fungicide, rated by the World Health Organisation as 'moderately hazardous'. It is highly toxic if swallowed and is an anticholinesterase compound. Pyrazophos is a mutagen. It is dangerous to bees and harmful to livestock, birds, animals and fish. A harvest interval of two weeks is set for hops and apples, and livestock should be kept out of treated areas for two weeks.

Pyrethrins An insecticide for household and garden use, and a wood preservative. The pyrethrins are the active ingredients in the plant-derived insecticide pyrethrum. The World Health Organisation considers these compounds to be 'moderately hazardous'. Pyrethrins are moderately toxic if swallowed: a dose of fifteen grams has proved fatal to a child. Once taken in, however, the chemicals are rapidly detoxified and passed out of the body. Some people may show allergic reactions, including contact dermatitis. These compounds are highly toxic to fish.

Pyrethroids A group of insecticides. They are synthetic chemicals based on the formula of the plant product **pyrethrum**. As the dangers of the earlier **organochlorine** and **organophosphorus** insecticides have become more apparent and their use has become progressively more restricted, pyrethroids have been marketed in increasing quantities. Their persistence is generally brief to moderate and some have marked advantages over other chemicals, e.g. **permethrin** and others are considered safe woodworm treatments for use in bat-inhabited roofs. They should still be treated with caution however. Their toxicity to humans may be high, some are known or suspected carcinogens in animals and some are allergens or irritants. They are not selective in their action and are therefore dangerous to bees and other beneficial insects and they are generally highly toxic to fish.

Pyrethrum Insecticide for household and garden use. Pyrethrum is moderately toxic if swallowed or inhaled. It is an irritant and may cause allergic dermatitis or asthmatic breathing in sensitive people. Pyrethrum is rapidly detoxified and no long-term health risks are known apart from the possibility of sensitisation to the substance. Pyrethrum is a 'knock-down' insecticide, acting very quickly but possibly allowing the insects to recover; for this reason it is often mixed with other insecticides or with **piperonyl butoxide**. Its persistence in the environment is very brief and it is one of the safest insecticides to use when bees are in the area. It is however highly toxic to fish. Pyrethrum is one of the very few insecticides the use of which may, in certain circumstances, be permitted within the organic standards set by the Soil Association.

Quassia The bark of a tropical American tree. An infusion of quassia chips is a relatively weak and non-persistent insecticide. Large doses can produce nausea if swallowed, but its toxicity is very low and weak solutions are used medicinally. We have no information on its environmental effects but the same precautions should be taken as with any pesticide (see page 53). It is reputed to be safe for bees.

Quaternary ammonium compounds (QACs) Chemicals based on nitrogen having a wide variety of uses. The toxicities of quaternary ammonium compounds vary greatly, from **paraquat** at the high end to common antiseptics such as cetrimide at the other. The commonest use for unspecified quaternary ammonium compounds is as fungicides and mould inhibitors in such products as patio cleaners, masonry biocides and wallpaper pastes. These are likely to be harmful if swallowed, though not highly toxic. They may cause skin irritation, so keep them off the skin and out of your eyes.

Red lead See Lead.

Resmethrin A **pyrethroid** insecticide for garden and indoor use. Its toxicity is moderate to high; inhalation is more likely to be harmful than swallowing and skin absorption may also be a problem. The World Health Organisation list it as 'slightly hazardous'. It is harmful to fish and bees.

Rotenone An insecticide. Rotenone is the active chemical ingredient in derris, a traditional insecticide of plant origin. It is highly toxic by swallowing or inhalation, the estimated fatal dose for an adult being ten to fifteen grams. There are however no records of any deaths, as large quantities are quickly ejected by vomiting. The World Health Organisation rate this compound as 'moderately hazardous'. It is a suspected animal carcinogen and has led to liver and kidney damage and reproductive effects at high doses in animal experiments. It is an irritant of the eyes and breathing passages and there is a risk of mild rashes if it is not kept off the skin. It is reported to be toxic to birds and animals, pigs in particular, potentially harmful to bees and highly toxic to fish. It breaks down fairly quickly in the environment and its occasional use in organic farming is permitted by the Soil Association.

Selenium sulphide An anti-dandruff compound. Selenium compounds are generally highly toxic but selenium sulphide is less dangerous than many of the others because of its low solubility. However it is toxic if swallowed and can be absorbed through the skin. It is a suspected animal carcinogen. When using a selenium sulphide shampoo do not swallow any of the material. Keep it out of your eyes, do not use if your scalp has any broken skin and do not use it in the bath as excessive quantities may be absorbed if you do.

Silica A mineral found in many rocks and some building materials. Silica is not especially toxic but its dust is dangerous if inhaled and in the long term gives rise to a lung disease called silicosis. Quarry workers and stone cutters are at risk from this, especially those working with granite. Exposure in the home is unlikely to be long enough to cause silicosis but if you are drilling or grinding much mineral-based material it is sensible to wear a dust mask.

Silica gel A compound used to attract water from the atmosphere to reduce humidity. The toxicity of silica gel is slight but it may cause some irritation if handled in the dried state.

Silicones Inert organic compounds of silicon. Silicones are used as lubricants and sealants for a variety of purposes, the main household use being in bath sealants. Once cured they are inert and harmless, although they may give off irritant fumes if burnt. While curing they release **acetic acid** vapour, which is an irritant.

Simazine A **weedkiller**. Simazine is classed as a residual herbicide and is used for keeping paths and drives clear, as the chemical remains effective for many months. It is very widely used by local authorities, British Rail and others. The World Health Organisation consider that simazine is 'unlikely to present an acute hazard in normal use'. The chemical has low toxicity. It is reported to be a mutagen and a weak animal carcinogen in laboratory tests. Some formulations may be irritant to the eyes and skin. Simazine is weakly toxic to fish and reduces populations of earthworms for three or four months after use. The main problem with simazine is its persistence in the water environment: watercourses and water supplies in many parts of England have become contaminated with this chemical. In some cases EEC limits on pesticides in drinking water have been exceeded. Simazine is on the government's draft 'red list' of toxic and persistent chemicals whose input to the water environment must be reduced, and it is difficult to see how this can be achieved without severe restrictions on its future use.

Sodium carbonate (washing soda) This chemical is a mild alkali. It is moderately toxic if swallowed and a skin and eye irritant. It should not be used to clean anything made of aluminium, as it may attack the surface of the metal. Prolonged contact with strong solutions can remove the outer skin layer. Wear gloves if you are using strong solutions and keep splashes out of your eyes.

Sodium chlorate A **weedkiller**, rated by the World Health Organisation as 'slightly hazardous'. It is very toxic if swallowed: fifteen grams can be fatal for an adult, three grams for a child. The chemical is an irritant if spilt onto the eyes or skin or if breathed in. It is a mutagen. Sodium chlorate is an oxidising agent and if spilt onto paper, rags or wood will make them highly inflammable. It is persistent in the soil and should not be allowed to contaminate water. It has been banned in Thailand.

Sodium hydrogen sulphate (sodium bisulphate) This is an acidic chemical used in some toilet cleaners. Once it becomes moist, it produces a dilute solution of **sulphuric acid**. It is therefore a potentially serious irritant of the skin, eyes and mucous membranes. When using powdered toilet cleaners do not breathe the dust or mist produced and wash any splashes off your skin at once with plenty of water. If you get dust in your eyes, wash them out thoroughly and seek medical attention if they still hurt. It is most important that products of this kind are never used at the same time as bleach, as the two chemicals will react rapidly to produce quantities of highly toxic **chlorine** gas.

Sodium hydroxide (caustic soda) A caustic alkali, used in some **oven cleaners** and **drain cleaners**. It is corrosive, highly toxic if swallowed and a serious skin and eye irritant even in dilute forms. It can cause an irritant dermatitis. The chemical has been found to be mutagenic. It is very harmful to aquatic life. It may react violently with acids or aluminium. If you should get any sodium hydroxide in your eyes you should immediately wash them in cold water for fifteen minutes while someone calls a doctor. Aerosols containing this chemical are very dangerous and should be avoided. Do not mix with **ammonia** solution, as large quantities of ammonia gas will be released.

Sodium hypochlorite Bleach. This chemical reacts slowly with water to produce reactive oxygen, an effective agent against bacteria. It is corrosive, dangerous if swallowed and irritant if inhaled. It is a mutagen. Although it degrades fully in time, its action against bacteria persists after it has been washed away. It should not be used where toilets or sinks drain into septic tanks, nor in outside drains that may empty into watercourses, and should be used sparingly anywhere else, as sewage treatment works rely on bacterial processes to break down wastes. Take care never to mix bleach with any acid product (which includes some toilet cleaners — see Sodium hydrogen sulphate) as the result will be a violent chemical reaction producing clouds of highly toxic **chlorine** gas.

Sodium metabisulphite A **sterilising agent**, used in home brewing and wine making, etc. The chemical decomposes in the presence of water to produce fumes of **sulphur dioxide**, an irritant gas that is usually first detected by its metallic taste rather than by smell. Higher concentrations are irritating to the eyes, then to the mucous membranes, dangerously so if exposure to the gas persists. Sodium metabisulphite is moderately toxic if swallowed. On heating, it decomposes rapidly and gives off sulphur dioxide.

Sodium pentachlorophenate See Pentachlorophenol.

Sodium percarbonate A mild bleach and cleaning compound, also contained in some **detergent powders** and **stain removers**. Sodium percarbonate is toxic if swallowed or inhaled and is an irritant. It decomposes when moist to produce hydrogen peroxide, which is a bleaching agent. Keep it off your skin, out of your eyes and wash splashes off immediately. Discard any that becomes moist or contaminated with other material.

Sodium phenylphenate (or phenoxide) See 2-phenylphenol.

Sodium tetraborate See Boric acids.

Solvents A general term for liquids which dissolve other materials. Solvents have many uses in adhesives, paints, cleaning products and other applications and a wide range of substances fall into this category. Some general points can be made about solvents. Many are toxic by inhalation (and quite a few are exploited by solvent abusers for this reason) and solvents are often absorbed through the skin. Inhalation effects often include dizziness and light-headedness, sometimes followed by sleepiness (narcosis). Liver and kidney disease sometimes follow prolonged exposure to solvents and many of these materials are inflammable. One study has shown a link between birth defects in babies and the mothers' exposure to solvents, but it was not always possible to identify which solvents were involved. As a general rule you should avoid breathing solvent vapours where possible and take precautions against fire.

Spirits of salts See Hydrochloric acid.

Styrene A solvent used in two-part fillers etc. Styrene is highly toxic if swallowed, moderately so if inhaled. It is a skin irritant. At high concentrations, the vapour is highly irritating to the eyes and the chemical has caused severe eye injuries; it also has narcotic properties and chronic exposure may affect the central nervous system. It is a mutagen and a possible animal carcinogen. The hazards of styrene are relatively low because it is less volatile than many other solvents and the vapours do not reach toxic concentrations so easily. You must, however, ensure adequate ventilation when using it as with any solvent.

Sulphamic acid Used as a kettle descaler. It is a moderately toxic compound if swallowed. It is irritating to the eyes and skin. It may emit toxic fumes on heating.

Sulphur A fungicide for use as a dust on plants. Sulphur has very low toxicity. It is an irritant however, very low concentrations of the dust in air being sufficient to irritate the eyes. With longer exposure, the dust may also become irritating to the mucous membranes if repeatedly breathed in. It may react or form dangerous mixtures with oxidisers (as in gunpowder for example) and if burnt it gives off toxic fumes of sulphur oxides.

Sulphur dioxide A gas used as a sterilant and food preservative (see Sodium metabisulphite). Sulphur dioxide is one of the most widespread and serious air pollutants in urban areas of the world. Millions of tons are poured into the atmosphere every year from the burning of coal and oil (which contain a certain amount of sulphur). Sulphur dioxide as a pollutant can be a threat to human health, especially for sufferers of chronic respiratory complaints such as bronchitis, and may also damage buildings and plants. There may be synergies between sulphur dioxide and smoke, **ozone**, or other pollutants. As a result of the Clean Air Acts, levels of sulphur dioxide in British cities have been reduced by two-thirds or more over the last thirty years. Once in the atmosphere, sulphur dioxide undergoes complex chemical reactions with **nitrogen oxides** and other air pollutants, the end results of which are sulphates and **sulphuric acid**. Sulphates as an air pollutant may adversely affect the health of sensitive people. They also form a fine haze which reduces visibility, especially during calm sunny weather. Sulphuric acid, dissolved in cloud and rain water, is the chief acidifying ingredient of acid rain.

Nearly all large urban areas in Britain are now 'smokeless zones', as set up by the Clean Air Acts, and this means it is an offence to burn solid fuels other than those of the approved kind, e.g. **coke**, Coalite and anthracite, all of which are fuels with a low sulphur content. The sulphur content of heating oils varies considerably according to their source. Natural gas is a low-sulphur fuel. Improving the energy efficiency of your household reduces your contribution to air pollution whichever fuel you use!

Sulphuric acid A strong acid, used as **battery acid**. Sulphuric acid is a dangerous and corrosive chemical. In concentrated form it is extremely corrosive and toxic to tissue, causing severe burns instantaneously on contact. It is a very strong oxidiser and may ignite organic compounds such as sugar. Dilute solutions, such as battery acid, are still strong enough to cause burns on the skin and would be very toxic if swallowed. Repeated contact with dilute solutions can also cause dermatitis. Repeated or prolonged inhalation of sulphuric acid mists inflames the upper respiratory tract and can cause bronchitis.

Synergised pyrethrins, synergised pyrethrum An **Insecticide**: pyrethrum or pyrethrins with another chemical added to increase their efficacy. See Piperonyl butoxide.

2,4,5-T A **herbicide**, widely used in the past as a brush-killer, now available in only one product (May & Baker's 'Kilnet'). 2,4,5-T has become one of the most controversial of all pesticides, following its use in the Vietnam war ('Agent Orange'). The World Health Organisation rating for this chemical is 'moderately hazardous'. It is highly toxic if swallowed. In animal experiments, it is a suspected carcinogen, teratogen and mutagen even in 'pure' formulations. 2,4,5-T is contaminated with very small amounts of extremely highly toxic TCDD (**dioxin**). It is harmful to fish. 2,4,5-T is banned in Colombia, Finland, Guatemala, India, Italy, Japan, the Netherlands, Norway, Russia, Sweden, Thailand and West Germany. In the UK it is banned by many local authorities and unions.

Tar oils A mixture containing **phenols** and other aromatic compounds, used as a 'winter wash' insecticide on **fruit trees**. It is very toxic if swallowed and an irritant to the skin and eyes; there is a risk of dermatitis, especially if it is used in sunlight. Tar products are weakly carcinogenic, and tar oils are dangerous to fish.

2,3,6-TBA A **herbicide** used in 'touchweeders'. The World Health Organisation rate this chemical as 'slightly hazardous'. It is moderately toxic if swallowed. The chemical can contain nitrosamine contaminants, which are possible carcinogens. It can be irritating to the eyes, skin and mucous membranes. Some products have been withdrawn in the USA. It is harmful to fish.

TBTO See Tributyltin oxide.

TCDD See Dioxins.

Tecnazene This compound is used as a fumigant **fungicide** and a treatment of potatoes in store to keep them from sprouting; it may be found as a pesticide residue in food. According to the World Health Organisation, it is 'unlikely to present a hazard in normal use'. It is a possible animal carcinogen. Skin sensitisation has occurred in some workers using this chemical. Toxic fumes are given off if tecnazene is heated. It is persistent in the environment and harmful to fish. If tecnazene is used as a greenhouse smoke, then no edible crop should be harvested for at least two weeks after use.

Tetrachloroethylene See Perchloroethylene.

Tetrachlorvinphos An **insecticide**, licensed for household pest control by professionals only. Little data available; it is of low toxicity and rapidly broken down. It is an **organophosphorus compound** and should therefore be presumed to be an anticholinesterase agent. It is highly toxic to fish.

Tetraethyl lead The principal lead additive to **petrol**. Tetraethyl lead is powerfully toxic by swallowing or inhalation. It is readily absorbed by the skin and a few drops on the skin can cause fatal poisoning. It dissolves readily in the fatty sheath that surrounds the nerves and hence causes rapid disruption to the workings of the brain and nervous system, leading to madness, convulsions and death. The amount of tetraethyl lead permitted in petrol has been reduced in recent years, and unleaded petrol is coming onto the market. This should always be used where possible, in order to reduce the amount of **lead** in the environment.

Tetrahydrofuran (THF) A powerful solvent, moderately toxic if swallowed or inhaled and narcotic in high concentrations. The chemical is irritating to the eyes and mucous membranes.

Chronic exposure is reported to have caused damage to liver and kidneys. THF is inflammable.

Tetramethrin A 'knock-down' **pyrethroid** insecticide for household and garden use, commonly used in aerosol sprays. According to the World Health Organisation it is 'unlikely to present an acute hazard in normal use'. It has slight to moderate toxicity if swallowed. Tetramethrin is dangerous to fish and toxic to bees.

Thiophanate-methyl A systemic **fungicide** used for the control of clubroot and other fungi in gardens. The World Health Organisation consider that this chemical is 'unlikely to present an acute hazard in normal use'. It is moderately toxic if swallowed. There is little to suggest any long-term hazard from the chemical itself, but once in the body, one of its breakdown products has been found to be carcinogenic, teratogenic and mutagenic. Several pests have developed resistance to thiophanate-methyl. Its use has been restricted in the USA and Finland.

Thiourea This chemical is found in one mole control product, along with **lindane** and **tecnazene**. It is a highly toxic chemical, especially if swallowed, and a carcinogen in animal experiments. It is reported to have had adverse effects on some women's blood and is said to affect the bone marrow with a consequent risk of anaemia. It has caused goitres in laboratory animals. It may cause severe allergic skin reactions.

Thiram A fungicide and yacht anti-fouling agent. The World Health Organisation rating for this chemical is 'slightly hazardous'. It is very toxic if swallowed. It is chemically similar to the drug disulfiram, which has a synergistic effect with alcohol, inducing instant nausea. Thiram is a possible animal carcinogen and teratogen and it is a mutagen in bacterial tests. Other long-term effects to which thiram has been linked include damage to the liver, nervous system and thyroid gland, and increased absorption of toxic metals. It may irritate the skin, eyes and breathing system; cases of contact dermatitis and allergic reaction have occurred. Thiram may produce poisonous gases on burning. It is moderately persistent, harmful to poultry and game, and toxic to fish. Harvest intervals vary from one to three weeks, depending on the crop.

Tin A metal, used as an ingredient in solder and as plating for food cans. It is not considered toxic.

Titanium dioxide A white pigment used in paints. It is a possible animal carcinogen and skin irritant. Its manufacture involves the production of large volumes of contaminated sludge, which has caused environmental problems.

Toluene A solvent used in damp treatments etc. and a major solvent in glues. It is moderately toxic if inhaled, less so if swallowed or absorbed through the skin. High concentrations may lead to narcosis, but this is unlikely to happen except through deliberate abuse. Long-term exposure may have psychological and central nervous system effects. It is mutagenic and a skin and eye irritant. Toluene is a slight fire hazard and produces irritant fumes on heating.

Triazines See Atrazine or simazine.

Tributyltin compounds These compounds were formerly contained in many yacht anti-fouling products. They are persistent marine pollutants and have caused severe damage to oyster beds and greatly reduced dogwhelk populations in many sheltered estuaries. TBT compounds were banned from use on small boats in July 1987, but are still permitted on larger ships.

Tributyltin oxide (TBTO) A wood preservative and masonry biocide. This compound is rated by the World Health Organisation as 'highly hazardous' and is highly toxic if swallowed. It may also be absorbed through the skin. It is an eye irritant. TBTO is suspected of attacking the immune system. It is a dangerous environmental pollutant (see **tributyltin compounds**). Products containing more than one per cent TBTO should not be available to householders.

Trichlorfon (Trichlorphon) An **organophosphorus** insecticide, listed by the World Health Organisation as 'slightly hazardous'. It is highly toxic if swallowed or inhaled and can be absorbed through the skin. It is an anticholinesterase compound. There is evidence for mutagenic effects and it is teratogenic and weakly carcinogenic in animals. Trichlorfon is highly irritating to the eyes. Long-term exposure to high doses may cause neurological damage. The chemical produces toxic fumes on heating. It is harmful to fish and may be toxic to bees. Its persistence is low and the minimum harvest interval is set at two days.

1,1,1-trichloroethane (methyl chloroform) A very widely used solvent. It is of low to moderate toxicity if swallowed or inhaled. In high concentrations it is narcotic and is sometimes deliberately inhaled. There are high risks in abusing this solvent: massive doses may lead to cardiac arrest and in the longer term it may cause psychological disturbance and affect the central nervous system. There is uncertain evidence for its carcinogenicity in animals. It is a mild skin irritant but severely irritant to the eyes. If you do get any in your eyes then rinse out with plenty of water and see a doctor if the irritation persists. Trichloroethane is very dangerous if partially burnt, as it forms highly toxic **phosgene** gas: do not use it where ther are naked lights and do not smoke in a room where it has been used. The chemical is persistent in the water environment and can be harmful in very low concentrations. It is also a potentially serious air pollutant, being one of the solvents that depletes the **ozone** layer. The release of trichloroethane into the air, whether indoors or out, should be kept to a minimum. Keep containers securely fastened when they are not actually in use, and prevent the build up of vapour in confined spaces by ensuring good ventilation.

Trichloroethylene ('trike') A solvent used in several DIY applications. It is highly toxic if inhaled, producing narcotic and anaesthetic effects, and cases of addiction have been recorded. Severe exposure to the fumes may lead to heart failure. There are many longer term hazards, including liver damage and psychological impairment (e.g. memory loss, depression). It is a mutagen, and a carcinogen and teratogen in animal experiments. The chemical has a low fire risk but produces toxic fumes if heated. It is a potentially serious contaminant of water supplies, leaching into underground aquifers where it persists and is difficult to remove.

Trichoderma spp A fungus. Used as a wood preservative and for treating trees. (See Fruit trees, page 62). No toxicity data found.

Triclopyr A translocated herbicide, sold as 'Garlon', amongst others. It is listed by the World Health Organisation as 'slightly hazardous'. It is a mild eye irritant and can be irritating to the skin. Triclopyr is dangerous to fish. Animals should be kept out of treated areas for at least seventeen days.

Triforine A fungicide. No safety data found, but the chemical has low toxicity if fed to rats.

Tri (hexylene glycol) biborate See Organoboron esters.

Turpentine A solvent, distilled from plant resins. Turpentine is highly toxic if inhaled and moderately toxic if swallowed. In the longer term it may damage the central nervous system and can cause serious irritation of the kidneys. It is a possible animal carcinogen. The substance is irritating to the skin and mucous membranes, and especially to the eyes. It is a moderate fire hazard: it does not catch alight easily but burns fiercely and with acrid smoke.

Turpentine substitute A hydrocarbon solvent. Turps substitute is a low-grade form of white spirit used for cleaning paint brushes and thinning paint. Its composition is variable but it is toxic if swallowed or inhaled. It can irritate the skin and may be carcinogenic depending on its composition (see also **hydrocarbons**). It is highly inflammable. Avoid excessive skin contact, do not breathe the vapour and take precautions against fire.

Vinyl chloride monomer (VCM) The raw material from which **PVC** is made. Vinyl chloride monomer is a known human carcinogen and may be present in most PVC products for some time after manufacture. It is released most quickly from thin products, e.g. sheets of PVC, but may remain longer in more solid items. To reduce the risk of cancer it may be advisable to ensure thorough ventilation after laying PVC tiles; lay them in summer when windows can be left open.

VOCs (volatile organic compounds) See Hydrocarbons.

Warfarin An anticoagulant **rat poison**. It is extremely toxic if swallowed and highly toxic if inhaled. According to the World Health Organisation warfarin is a 'slightly hazardous' chemical. It is a teratogen in animal experiments. This chemical must be stored and handled with great care, particularly if there is a risk that children or pets could get access to it. Baits must be placed so as to ensure that no pets can reach them. Warfarin is considerably less potent than the newer anticoagulants and the risk of secondary poisoning is correspondingly much lower. Rats have become resistant to warfarin in several parts of central and southern England, Wales and Southern Scotland. Anyone who suffers from haemophilia is particularly vulnerable to anticoagulant poisoning and should not use this substance nor any of the more modern rodenticides such as **difenacoum** and **bromadiolone**.

White spirit A hydrocarbon solvent used in paints and for washing paint brushes. White spirit is moderately toxic if swallowed or inhaled and can be absorbed through the skin. It can cause severe skin irritation on prolonged contact and some people may be sensitive to it. It is inflammable. Prolonged exposure to white spirit is thought to cause brain damage and other neurological symptoms and dermatitis has been reported. It contains varying amounts of aromatic compounds and may well be carcinogenic. Ensure thorough ventilation when using white spirit and avoid excessive skin contact. Take precautions against fire.

Xylene An aromatic hydrocarbon solvent. Xylene, of which there are three forms with broadly the same hazardous properties, is moderately toxic if inhaled or absorbed through the skin. It is a mild irritant and is highly inflammable. High concentrations of xylene vapour produce sleepiness. Prolonged exposure to xylene vapour has been found to cause nervous system effects such as tiredness, irritability, dizziness, light-headedness and agitation. Avoid excessive skin contact with xylene, ensure thorough ventilation and take precautions against fire.

Zinc A metal used as a protective coating for iron and steel and for flashings, gutters and similar applications. Zinc can be toxic in excessive doses and is harmful to plants. As normally used, however, it is unlikely to pose a hazard and on safety grounds is preferable to lead as a building material, although it does not last as long, especially in areas where the rain is acidic.

Zinc chromate An ingredient of some metal priming paints. No toxicity data have been found other than one report that zinc chromate is carcinogenic. Handle paints containing zinc chromate with care and avoid excessive skin contact as it may cause irritation. If sanding down painted surfaces (e.g. radiators) do not breathe the dust.

Zinc naphthenate This is a fungicide used in wood preservatives. Little information is available; what there is suggests that it is of low toxicity. It may be a fire risk in use. Zinc naphthenate is one of the chemicals that the Nature Conservancy Council consider safe to use in a roof where bats may roost or breed. The solvents used may however still be toxic to bats so treatment should not be carried out while they are likely to be using the roof.

Zinc phosphate An ingredient of metal priming paints. No toxicity data have been found. It is certain to be safer than the lead compounds that it replaces.

Zineb A yacht anti-fouling product. It is moderately toxic if swallowed or inhaled. The World Health Organisation list this chemical as 'unlikely to present an acute hazard in normal use'. Several chronic effects of the chemical have been recorded, including changes in the liver and anaemia in humans and thyroid changes in animals. It is a mutagen and a carcinogen in laboratory animals. Zineb is believed to be a reproductive hazard: exposed women workers in Russia are reported to have experienced a high level of spontaneous abortions. It has been linked with cases of skin, eye and mucous membrane irritation in exposed people and allergies among workers. It may be toxic to fish.

Ziram A component of yacht anti-fouling paint. Ziram is rated by the World Health Organisation as 'slightly hazardous'. The chemical is a mutagen and has shown some signs of genetic toxicity in workers exposed to it. It has caused irritation to the skin, eyes and mucous membranes. It is harmful to fish.

7.

FURTHER INFORMATION

Further information on the safety of chemicals described in this book can be obtained from a variety of sources. A useful initial step would be to contact the manufacturers and ask for the safety data sheet that they supply to people using the product in industry. You can also demand to know what harmful materials are in a particular product before you buy it, although you should not be surprised if the manufacturer refuses to tell you. Do not rely on the advice of the sales staff in the hardware or DIY shop — they may not have any more information about the product than appears on the label.

ORGANISATIONS

If you feel that a chemical product is being irresponsibly advertised then you may write and complain to the **Advertising Standards Authority**, Brook House, Torrington Place, London WC1E 7HN.

CLEAR, the Campaign for Lead-Free Air (3 Endsleigh Street, London WC1), can give advice on the conversion of cars to run on unleaded petrol and its availability in your area.

The **Consumers' Association** frequently covers domestic safety issues as well as reporting on the effectiveness of various products in its magazine *Which*. This is available on subscription and is also kept by many libraries.

The **Environmental Health Department** of your district council or London borough also has expertise in the area of chemicals safety and can check your home for asbestos or lead in paint if you suspect it is there. They can also advise you about the safe disposal of old chemicals, waste from paint stripping etc.

Foresight (The Old Vicarage, Church Lane, Whitley, Surrey GU8 5PN) offers advice on the avoidance of chemicals before and during pregnancy and has a number of leaflets available.

Friends of the Earth are actively campaigning on a wide range of environmental issues, including pesticide control and drinking water quality. They have a network of local groups — for details contact them at 26–28 Underwood Street, London N1 7JQ.

Greenpeace (30–31 Islington Green, London N1) also run campaigns on many issues, including toxic waste disposal and pollution of the seas.

The Health and Safety Executive, which has offices in several major cities, is responsible for enforcing the law on industrial safety. They should be able to advise you about the safe use of chemical products and they also publish a number of technical reports about the toxicity of chemicals and the safety precautions to be observed when using them. These are available from Her Majesty's Stationery Office and can be ordered through normal booksellers.

The **London Food Commission** (88 Old Street, London EC1) is a campaigning and research organisation concerned with pesticide residues on food, nitrates in drinking water and other issues concerning food quality and health. They publish *Food Magazine*.

The **London Hazards Centre**, Headland House, 308 Grays Inn Road, London WC1X 8DS. This organisation has considerable expertise in the field of dangerous chemicals and has published a number of reports, including a book on wood treatments (*Toxic Treatments* by Rory O'Neill). Hazards centres are also being set up in a number of other cities.

The **Marine Conservation Society** (9 Gloucester Road, Ross-on-Wye, Herefordshire) can give up-to-date advice on yacht anti-fouling paints.

The **National Society for Clean Air** (136 North Street, Brighton) has a wide range of material available on air pollution of all types, including indoor pollution from cookers, solvents etc. Their journal *Clean Air* is available in some reference libraries, and their Information Officer is happy to answer enquiries from the general public.

The **Nature Conservancy Council** (Northminster House,

Peterborough PE1 1UA) is a statutory body concerned with wildlife protection. They offer advice on timber treatments that are not harmful to bats.

The Pesticides Trust (c/o WUS, 20 Compton Terrace, London N1) is an independent research and information organisation dealing with pesticide hazards and alternatives.

Two organisations can give advice on gardening without pesticides or artificial fertiliers: **The Soil Association**, (86–88 Colston Street, Bristol BS1 5BB) and the **Henry Doubleday Research Association**, (Ryton-on-Dunsmore, Coventry CV8 3LG). Both have a range of publications that you may find useful.

The county council **Trading Standards Department** is responsible for monitoring toy safety and frequently analyses toy paint for toxic metals. They also have an interest in controlling other dangerous products and may be able to help if you have a specific problem in this area.

Your water authority or water company will normally be prepared to analyse your tap water for lead and should also tell you about other contaminants in your water supply. You may need to press them for detailed information but if they refuse to give it the local newspaper may well be interested.

If you suspect **wildlife** is being poisoned by the deliberate or accidental misuse of chemicals then there are a number of bodies who should be alerted. If water pollution is the problem then you should contact the water authority at once in order to get the pollution traced to its source and dealt with. Victims of poisoning may be cared for by the **RSPCA** (local branches in the telephone book). Corpses of predatory birds and animals may be sent to the **Institute of Terrestrial Ecology** (Monks Wood Experimental Station, Abbots Ripton, Huntingdon PE17 2LS) for post-mortem examination if they are still in a reasonable condition. The **Ministry of Agriculture** has a Veterinary Service that will deal with suspected poisoning incidents where domestic animals or livestock are concerned. Illegal use of poison baits is a police matter, but you may get a more diligent response from the **Royal Society for the Protection of Birds** (The Lodge, Sandy, Bedfordshire) if birds are the victims.

BOOKS AND JOURNALS

Several of the organisations listed above produce their own publications. In addition, the following books and journals may be useful sources of further information:

Books
Pesticide Users' Health and Safety Handbook by Andrew Watterson (Gower Technical Press).
The Green Consumer Guide by John Elkington and Julia Hailes (Gollancz).
The Earth Report, edited by Edward Goldsmith and Nicholas Hildyard (Mitchell Beazley).
The Friends of the Earth Handbook, (Friends of the Earth).
The Residue Report by Stephanie Lashford (Thorsons).
Chemicals and Society by Hugh Crone (Cambridge University Press).
The Poisoned Womb by John Elkington (Viking).
The Toxic Metals by Anthony Tucker (Earth Island, now out of print).
The Hole in the Sky by John Gribbin (Corgi).

Journals
ENDS Report — a useful monthly summary of environmental issues, regulations and policies. (Environmental Data Services Ltd., Finsbury Business Centre, 40 Bowling Green Lane, London EC1R 0NE).
New Scientist
The Ecologist
London Environment Bulletin
Environment Now

Readers wishing to study environmental topics in more depth may find the Open University course 'Environmental Control and Public Health' of interest.

BIBLIOGRAPHY

The information contained in this book was obtained, in the main, from the following sources.

Adhesives Directory 1987.
British Medical Journal.
Chemistry in Britain.
Curwell, S. R. and March, C. G., *Hazardous Building Materials.* Spon
Dudley, N. *Garden Pesticides.* The Soil Association.
Environmental Science and Technology.
Fletcher, A. C. *Reproductive Hazards of Work.* Equal Opportunities Commission.
Hazards Bulletin.
The Health and Safety Executive. *Toxicity Reviews,* HMSO.
Hunter, D. *The Diseases of Occupations,* English Universities' Press.
The Lancet.
Lees, A. and McVeigh, K. *An Investigation of Pesticide Pollution in Drinking Water in England and Wales,* Friends of the Earth.
The McGraw-Hill Encyclopaedia of Science and Technology, McGraw-Hill.
Ministry of Agriculture, Fisheries and Food, and the Health and Safety Executive. Reference Book 500, *Pesticides 1988.* HMSO.
New Scientist.
Nordberg, G. F. *Effects and Dose–Response Relationship of Toxic Metals.* Elsevier.
O'Niell, L. A., *Health and Safety, Environmental Pollution and the Paint Industry,* Paint Research Association.
Rutter, M. and Russell-Jones, R. J. *Lead and Health,* John Wiley.
Sax, N. Irving (ed.) *Dangerous Properties of Industrial Materials.* Van Nostrand-Reinhold.
Shawyer, C. R. *The Barn Owl in the British Isles, Its Past, Present and Future.* The Hawk Trust.
Turner, G. P. A. *Introduction to Paint Chemistry* (Chapman Hall).
US National Institute of Occupational Safety and Health Toxic Substances List. National Institute of Occupational Safety and Health.
Watterson, A. *Pesticide Users' Health and Safety Handbook,* Gower Press.

APPENDIX

Chemicals for which there is evidence of carcinogenic effects
Key
An ?   — possible/suspected carcinogen in animal experiments.
An + — confirmed carcinogen in animal experiments.
Hu ? — suspected human carcinogen.
Hu + — confirmed human carcinogen.
?   — reference ambiguous.

An entry in brackets refers only to some chemicals in a group, not necessarily to all of them.

Aminotriazole	Hu ?	Mancozeb	An +
Aromatic compounds	(Hu +)	Naphthalene	An ?
Arsenic compounds	(Hu +)	Nicotine	An +
Asbestos	Hu +	Nitrosamines	An + Human ?
Benomyl	An ?	NTA	An +
Benzene	Hu +	Paradichlorobenzene	An ?
Bitumen	Hu +	Pentachlorophenol	An ?
Cadmium	Hu ?	Pepper	An +
Calcium plumbate	?	Perchloroethylene	An +
Captan	An +	Permethrin	?
Carbamates	(An +)	Piperonyl butoxide	An +
Carbaryl	An +	Plasticisers	(An +)
Carbendazim	An +	PCBs	Hu ?
Carbon tetrachloride	?	PAHs	(Hu ?)
Chlordane	Hu ?	Polystyrene	An +
Chlorinated hydrocarbons	(Hu +)	Polyurethane	An +
Coal, combustion products of	(Hu ?)	Pyrethroids	(An +)
Copper sulphate	An ?	Rotenone	An ?
Creosote	Hu +	Selenium sulphide	An ?
Cypermethrin	An +	Simazine	An +
2,4-D	An + Human ?	Styrene	An ?
Dibromoethane	?	2,4,5-T	An ?
Dichloromethane	An +	Tar oils	Hu +
Dichlorvos	Hu ?	Tecnazene	An ?
Dieldrin	An +	Thiourea	An +
Diethylene glycol	An +	Thiram	An ?
Dimethoate	An +	Titanium dioxide	An ?
Dinocap	An ?	Trichlorfon	An +
Dioxins	An + Human ?	1,1,1-trichloroethane	An ?
Diuron	An ?	Trichloroethylene	An +
Formaldehyde	An + Human ?	Turpentine	An ?
Gamma HCH	An + Human ?	Turps substitute	?
Hydrocarbons	(Hu +)	Vinyl chloride	Hum +
Limonene	An ?	White spirit	?
Malathion	An ?	Zinc chromate	?
Maleic hydrazide	An ?	Zineb	An +

INDEX

This index lists, in the main, only items which do not have an alphabetical listing in the appropriate section of the book.

180 *Index*

GREEN PRINT is an imprint of the Merlin Press, addressing issues raised by the green and environmental movements. Our early titles have included:

LIVING WITHOUT CRUELTY by Mark Gold
THE RACE FOR RICHES by Jeremy Seabrook
THE STOLEN FUTURE by Patrick Rivers
INTO THE 21ST CENTURY edited by Felix Dodds
FAR FROM PARADISE by John Seymour and Herbert Girardet
AFTER THE CRASH by Guy Dauncey
DEVELOPED TO DEATH by Ted Trainer
THE GREEN GUIDE TO ENGLAND by John Button
THE VEGETARIAN HOLIDAY AND RESTAURANT GUIDE by Peter and Pauline Davies
C FOR CHEMICALS by Michael Birkin and Brian Price
CHICKEN AND EGG by Clare Druce

All royalties from our colour cookery book, THE CELEBRITY VEGETARIAN COOKBOOK, edited by Geoff Francis and Janet Hunt, go to the Sarvodaya leaf protein project in Sri Lanka.

Green Print books are available from any bookshop, or from the publishers. If you have difficulty obtaining our books, please let us know. For a catalogue, and to join our free mailing list, write to **Green Print (ML), The Merlin Press, 10 Malden Road, London NW5 3HR.** We'll be glad to hear from you, and to know what you think of our books.